SENSORY DIVERSITY

The MATTERS Approach to Living in a Neurotypical World with a Neurodivergent Body

by Shaylynn Hayes-Raymond

Published by Sensory Education
Oromocto, Canada

Cover Art and Print/eBook design
by Imperceptions Press

Edited by Harrison Porter

ISBN: 978-1-990467-58-5

Dedicated to all of us who are neurodivergent living in a world designed for neurotypicals, and to the following:

To Preston Raymond, my husband and best friend: Thank you for your endless support.

To my mother Michelle Hayes, and my father Roddie Hayes: Thank you for believing in me.

To Dr. Jennifer Jo Brout: Thank you for guiding me along this path and teaching me about the sensory world and your contributions to the field.

To Susan Nesbit: Thank you for your explanations of the history of sensory processing.

To Amber Liponoga, Harrison Porter, Scott Wright, and Sharon Mousel-Burns: Thank you for joining me for this journey and your continued support.

Contents

Introduction

My name is Shaylynn Hayes-Raymond, and I am a counsellor in New Brunswick, Canada. I have been an advocate for misophonia and sensory dysregulation since learning about the condition in 2014 when I wrote and published my first book on the subject, *Full of Sound and Fury: Living with Misophonia.* My interest in sensory dysregulation and learning more about it came to fruition through personal experience. Almost suddenly at age 19, I began to react to the world around me differently, whereby I was confused and frustrated by the tumultuous fight-flight-freeze experience I had when faced with otherwise normal stimuli such as legs shaking, whistling, tapping, and pens clicking. I did not know it at the time, but I would soon find out that I was suffering from something called misophonia—which I now view as part of a larger pattern of sensory dysregulation. After learning about the condition, as well as the lack of research and awareness on the subject, I became dedicated to the cause.

After graduating with a Bachelor of Arts in Political Science, I undertook my Master of Arts in Counselling Psychology. I was driven to complete this degree and become a counsellor because I wanted to help persons with misophonia like myself. I will say that several professors throughout my degree mentioned that I was hyper-focused on misophonia. Some believed I should be less focused on one condition, but at my core, misophonia was the *reason* why I was there, and was the reason why I felt so passionate about undertaking a career in the counselling profession. Today I am the Director of The International Misophonia Foundation, run a private practice for therapy, and offer coaching coping sessions worldwide for persons with misophonia and sensory dysregulation. I am now dedicated to the larger picture of sensory dysregulation through the "Sensory Diversity" movement (sensorydiversity.com). I am also passionate about providing education and resources to clinicians interested in supporting those with sensory dysregulation.

Much of my work involves talking to people with sensory dysregulation and seeing what helps them, assessing my own coping strategies, and taking a compassionate approach which understands that persons with sensory dysregulation are not simply lacking control of their emotions and behaviours, but are instead subject to a very real, very disorienting, physiological response.

This book provides a transdiagnostic multisensory approach to neurodivergence. You will not find specific sections isolated for Misophonia, Autism, or ADHD; instead, we explore the shared sensory and emotional experiences that are common across neurodivergent communities and experiences. The purpose of this book is to explore the world from the perspective of a neurodivergent person navigating a neurotypical world.

What Does It Mean to be Neurodivergent?

Both the social and medical models of mental and neurological health aim to define neurodivergence. In my opinion, both of these models fall short because neurodivergence encapsulates many discrete and co-occurring phenomena. Primarily, when we speak of neurodivergence we refer to autism, sensory processing disorder/sensory integration, ADHD, Dyslexia, Dysgraphia, and Dyscalculia, Tourette's, tic disorders, vestibular disorders, and misophonia. Some frameworks of neurodivergence include Bipolar Disorder, OCD, and CPTSD. This is not an exhaustive list and it may grow over time as different perspectives emerge. Even as awareness for neurodivergent conditions rises, many are still left without a concrete understanding of the neurodivergent world.

To put it simply, neurodivergence is any state of being that is not *neurotypical—the expected human behaviour, emotional processing, and sensory processing state*. However, it is entirely possible that there is no such thing as "neurotypical" and there may instead be a wider range of neurodiversity with some individuals landing where we would have traditionally called it "typical". The variation in different brains is something that is up for debate—but regardless, for those we currently call neurodivergent, these variations can make navigating a world designed for different nervous systems challenging.

While the "spectrum" has been a useful way to explain the differences between autistic or sensory individuals, this has led to some confusion and misinterpretation where people believe that "everyone is on a *spectrum"*.

On a practical level, autism refers to a neurodevelopmental difference in individuals who may also experience sensory processing challenges, under-responsivity, social and cognitive differences, and more. Persons with sensory integration or sensory processing issues can be autistic, or they can have these differences discreetly. Vestibular disorders relate to movement and our perception of the world around us. ADHD is a cognitive and sensory-based condition where dysregulation of the executive functions occurs, and misophonia refers to an extreme sensory reaction where sounds cause a fight-flight-freeze response in individuals. The trouble in understanding comes from the consistent overlap in individuals—some may have one or all of these criteria. I am being careful not to refer to this as a *diagnosis* or *condition* that one has, as I am cognizant of the preference of many individuals, especially when regarding autism, to think more in terms of identity and community.

To be neurodivergent is to experience the world in a way that is not *typical* historically and is thus a culturally diverse experience. This book will focus primarily on sensory diversity and navigating a neurotypical world with a neurodivergent body. However, *neurodiversity* is a much more fitting name for the experience of every brain being different. In the case of this book, I will refer to neurodivergence as a *divergence from common neurological and cognitive realities*. This term is not meant to pass judgement on individuals who are neurodivergent, but rather, to explain the various differences that lead to friction for those whom the system was not designed for. While I do think it is important to note that neurodiversity is a broad term, and that neurodivergence has the potential to be taken as an "other" or "flaw", I think it is important to distinguish these differences to highlight personal experiences and the need for neuroinclusive and sensory-diverse spaces.

What is the MATTERS Approach?

Multisensory **A**dvocacy **T**ailored **T**herapeutic **E**motion **R**egulation **S**upport

I initially created the MATTERS approach with misophonia in mind. Over time, I came to realize that the coping skills I was using for misophonia were also helping me with depression, OCD, and anxiety. I will say that it is possible that through helping one condition, the others are more easily managed. However, I think there are also instances such as ADHD, autism, trauma, and other conditions where a multisensory advocacy approach can help improve one's quality of life. During my graduate program in Master of Arts in Counselling Psychology, I became even more disenchanted with the cognitive behavioural one-size-fits-all approach to counselling and understanding the human brain and behaviour. I do not think that humans are just what we do, but are rather a cumulation of emotions, thoughts, feelings, and chemical compositions that can manifest in completely different ways.

The idea of a MATTERS approach is twofold. For one, the word is an anagram for the program itself, and two, focusing on our mental and neurophysiological traits is something that matters. It is, of course, what makes us human beings. While diagnostic tests exist for numerous mental and neurobiological conditions, I think it is far more important to focus on individual traits, expressions, and ideas for what constitutes a condition. Rather than focus on a client "having" a condition, the matters approach is agnostic to diagnosis. Whatever problems that are facing the individual, whether it is struggling in their own brain in the world, addiction, trauma, or depression, the matters approach is designed to consider these differences. This is not to say that medical attention is not important: psychiatric patients should obviously listen to their psychiatrists, and persons with seizures should listen to their medical doctors. What this does say is that no matter the diagnosis or prognosis, the matters approach lives outside of that paradigm and instead utilizes advocacy, psychoeducation, self-regulation, and appropriate cognitive and behavioural strategies.

One thing I find incredibly uncomfortable about psychotherapy and counselling is the use of the term "intervention". The use of this term is infantilizing. People who are struggling are reduced to the role of a misbehaved child. Instead of figuring out the neurophysiological basis for their choices, or even exploring their emotional motivations outside of the characteristics of the DSM, we are left with bullet points on a medical chart. I found myself cringing every time I heard this word throughout my program. "What intervention is your favourite?" was a common question, and my eyes would glaze over and I would simply reply, "I do not have one, definitely not CBT."

Many conditions are more complex and less understood than the headlines on social media clickbait websites would have you believe. Psychology as a discipline is as old as humanity, and yet, also as young as the last two centuries. There is also a social construct to mental illness and depending on your culture you may have a stigma against the idea that there are problems in the brain that the spirit cannot overcome. For me, the answer to the question of "what are we" is far more complex and not something that any scientist, psychologist, counsellor, priest, shaman, or philosopher will ever know the answer to, and if they did, how boring would life be? So—if this question is so timeless, and so unanswered, why are we willing to hinge the very being of a human on the idea of a diagnostic criteria?

I am not here to say that every condition, behaviour, or human experience is due to their sensory systems, or even that mental illnesses and psychiatric conditions do not exist. That would be a throw-the-baby-out-with-the-bathwater argument, and that is not the point at all. For some people, their emotional regulation problems stem from behaviour or personal experiences outside of their neurophysiological state. This is entirely consistent with the MATTERS approach since one should always consider the individual above all else. Psychoeducation and academic research are heavily embraced in the MATTERS perspective. One should always be seeking information and learning more about these conditions, and assuming matters are settled and sticking to old conceptualizations of disorders is just as bad as never believing the person has a disorder in the first place. Clinicians use diagnostic tools to help identify which courses of action might be helpful to their client or patient. This is not an unimportant part of psychiatric and psychological care, but it should always be viewed through the lens of limitations. It should also always be considered that labels can come with stigma attached.

Multisensory **A**dvocacy **T**ailored **T**herapeutic **E**motion **R**egulation **S**upport

Multisensory: The MATTERS approach views the human condition as a multisensory experience. While the MATTERS approach is transdiagnostic and neuro-affirming, it does not specifically follow a social-only model, but rather blends the social model with a medical model supported by modern neuroscience and personal experiences of those with conditions.

Advocacy: Advocacy in the MATTERS approach views self-advocacy and community advocacy, including accommodations, as a necessary part of coping with mental or neurological illnesses. Advocacy can include changing the world around you in your home, school, work, community, and more. Advocacy is also a powerful tool for taking ownership of one's personal experiences and sharing experiences with others, such as through writing, presenting, video-making, and more.

Tailored: As a framework rather than a specific model, the MATTERS approach should be tailored to each individual client and their families. This aspect thus contains significant variability. Every part of the MATTERS approach should be tailored to the individual needs of the client—whether that is the multi-sensory aspect, advocacy, therapeutic choices, emotional choices, regulation, and support.

Therapeutic: The therapeutic aspect of MATTERS ensures that clinicians using these approaches are working under a lens of psychotherapy. Rather than throwing an approach to the wall and seeing what sticks, a lens of psychotherapy is required to enact the MATTERS approach. While this approach can be varied, it is important that the therapeutic choices align with modern literature and evidence-based practice. Approaches such as CBT, DBT, ACT, Gestalt therapy, play therapy, narrative therapy, and others are consistent with the MATTERS approach so long as the multisensory component and specific social and biological needs of the client are met. This includes, for example, the choice of not using exposure therapy for conditions such as misophonia where exposure makes things worse.

Emotion: Emotion is more than just a 'thought' or a 'feeling' in the MATTERS approach. Emotions, instead, are an aggregate of our biological composition, life experiences, current biological state, and environmental factors. The emotional part of MATTERS should thus focus on a multisensory approach.

Regulation: In the MATTERS approach, regulation is an important part of ensuring that clients are able to participate in sessions as well as navigate their daily lives with their conditions. The goals of regulation can be supported by other areas of the MATTERS approach.

Support: Support is an ongoing commitment in the MATTERS approach to client wellness and sustainable progress. This framework recognizes that while shorter forms of therapy can be beneficial, an ongoing supportive figure or community can be important to sustaining positive outcomes. Whether this is through regular check-ins, the availability of email, or through social communities of peers, this support is an essential part of the process. Support can also come in the form of letters of accommodation written by a therapist.

[illegible] biological [illegible] [illegible] [illegible] [illegible] [illegible] RS [illegible] [illegible] [illegible] approach.

[illegible] [illegible] [illegible] [illegible] [illegible] [illegible] [illegible] [illegible] [illegible] [illegible] [illegible] [illegible] [illegible]

[illegible] support is an ongoing commitment in [illegible] [illegible] RS approach [illegible] and [illegible] progress. This framework recognizes [illegible] [illegible] [illegible] [illegible] [illegible] [illegible] [illegible] [illegible] [illegible] [illegible] [illegible] [illegible] this support is an essential part of the process. Support can also come in the form of letters of encouragement written by a mentor.

What are our Senses?

One of the first things we learn in kindergarten or elementary school is that we have five senses. These senses are often described as sight, smell, touch, taste, and hearing. However, there are more accurately eight senses—and there could be more yet to be discovered. The final three senses that are most often mentioned in literature on sensory processing and integration are the following: proprioception, interoception, and vestibular.

Proprioception refers to our brain's ability to connect with our muscles, tendons, and ligaments and send feedback on pressure and physical sensations that go beyond surface skin level tactile sensations. Proprioception is how we understand how our bodies are moving, such as *I am doing yoga* or, *I have moved my leg upwards.* Proprioception is commonly used to help those who are overwhelmed by sensory input by providing proprioceptive pressure such as a bear hug which can provide feedback to the body that it is feeling safe. The emotional aftermath of this proprioceptive pressure may differ from person to person.

Interoception refers to the body's ability to perceive what is going on *inside* of the body. The ability to know if one is hungry, tired, or in need of using the washroom are all examples of interoception. For example, I almost never feel *hungry* until my stomach is physically gargling. Interoception can be misinterpreted for psychological conditions like eating disorders as those who have difficulty with interoception can mimic these symptoms. Interoception can also complicate emotions by not providing accurate internal feedback. Hunger could be perceived as anxiety rather than a need to eat, and so on. Interoception regulation is an important part of supporting those with sensory needs.

The vestibular system refers to the body's ability to understand its own movement. As we shake our heads, we are engaging our vestibular systems. This system is also responsible for balance and our ability to perceive how our movements will interact with the environment. For those with vestibular issues, it can be difficult to view spinning items or movement such as icons on a computer screen, often leading to dizziness and even migraines. Inner ear complications can cause vestibular issues, but it is also possible to have vestibular issues due to sensory processing capabilities.

The History of Sensory Processing Research

For those outside of the occupational therapy community, it may come as a surprise that sensory research has been ongoing for multiple generations, starting with Dr. Jean Ayres in the 1970s. There is a rich and thorough history of sensory integration dysfunction which was later reconceptualized, perhaps wrongly, to sensory processing disorder. While sensory processing disorder has gained the most traction in the popular press and modern concepts of sensory processing, the seminal work of Jean Ayres must not be forgotten as we take in the field as a whole and understand the literature from its inception to present theories.

There is an unfortunate political side to academic writing. Camps begin to arise in literature as well as concepts and theories, and perhaps insidiously, scholarship can rewrite itself through renaming concepts and omitting either by design or accident key scholarly citations that should have prefaced the work. While there are countless academic and peer-reviewed studies published throughout the past half century, to make things easier I will be focusing on published books to help keep the list from overflowing and becoming confusing. The following is a timeline of prominent works on sensory integration/processing:

- Sensory Integration and Learning Disorders was published by Dr. Jean Ayres in 1972
- Sensory Integration and the Child was published by Dr. Jean Ayres in 1979
- The Out-of-Sync Child was published by Carol Stock Kranowitz in 1998
- Sensory Profile User's Manual was published by Dr. Winnie Dunn in 1999
- Sensational Kids: Hope and Help for Children with Sensory Processing Disorder was published by Dr. Lucy Jane Miller in 2006
- Living Sensationally: Understanding Your Senses was published by Dr. Winnie Dunn in 2007
- No Longer A Secret: Unique Common Sense Strategies for Children with Sensory or Motor Challenges was published by Doreit Bialer and Dr. Lucy Jane Miller in 2011

During the period from the 1980s to the 2010s, the research on sensory integration dysfunction and what Lucy Miller renamed sensory processing disorder was at its peak. Unfortunately, this splinter between views makes it harder to understand the larger picture of sensory processing. At present, neither Sensory Integration Dysfunction nor Sensory Processing Disorder are in the DSM or ICD. In my personal opinion, a lack of cohesion from research camps and conceptualization of sensory phenomenon has led to less general application of sensory-based conditions that are discrete from autism spectrum disorder, despite overlap and differentiation between those who have sensory processing difficulties without other characteristics of autism spectrum disorder.

The point of analyzing this history is not to pick sides, but rather to understand that sensory processing is neither new to literature, nor a settled area of expertise and understanding. All sensory practitioners and researchers operate through a lens that they have borrowed from those before them, with some taking more from sensory integration dysfunction and others taking more from sensory processing disorder. A third camp has taken parts of both and maintained that the truth to sensory processing may lie in the middle—with multiple experiences and perspectives necessary to grow the field. I personally have great respect for Dr. Jean Ayres, Winnie Dunn, Carol Kranowitz, and Lucy Miller. I believe it is important to consider the context of sensory processing literature that has come before us as we move into new areas of understanding and discovery. Rather than erasing the history of sensory processing, there is a rich and unique background for sensory processing that can help prevent modern researchers from starting fresh without any conceptual background for studying the phenomenon.

What is Sensory Diversity?

Sensory Diversity is the recognition that every individual perceives, filters, and responds to the world in a fundamentally unique way. While the vital movement for neurodiversity celebrates the different ways our brains process thought, sensory diversity focuses on the very gateway to those thoughts—our senses. It asserts that the world, both digital and physical, must be intentionally built to accommodate the full spectrum of human sensory experience.

Sensory diversity views our senses similarly to how neurodiversity views the brain. However, sensory diversity is focused widely on specific sensory processing of the world. While sensory dysregulation, the term I use for those who have sensory processing that is atypical, refers to a mismatch in sensory processing, neurodiversity refers to different brain types, including neurotypical and neurodivergent. In this view, sensory dysregulation is a form of neurodivergence.

For many neurodivergent individuals, the world is not merely a collection of experiences but a relentless barrage of sensory input that the nervous system must constantly negotiate. While neurotypical standards often dictate that we should be able to ignore the hum of a refrigerator, the fluorescent flicker of an office light, or the distant murmur of a crowded room, the reality for those with sensory processing differences is that these inputs are physically and emotionally taxing. We are often taught from a young age that resilience means enduring discomfort for the sake of social cohesion, yet true resilience often lies in the quiet radical act of honoring our physiological needs rather than suppressing them. This means moving away from the lingering grief of what we think our lives should look like and toward a functional acceptance of what they actually require to be sustainable and healthy.

The sensory aspect of neurodivergence is not a matter of preference, or a lack of discipline, or a sign of fragility, but rather a fundamental difference in how our brains filter and prioritize the environment. When the environment feels too loud, too bright, or too tactile, the body enters a state of high alert that can lead to profound exhaustion and long-term burnout. Recognizing this is the first step in dismantling the heavy guilt that often accompanies the need for accommodations. It is okay to choose the quiet path, to wear noise-canceling headphones in public, or to opt out of high-stakes social events that promise nothing but sensory overload. These choices are not failures of character or social inadequacies, but rather necessary adjustments for neurophysiological health. When we stop trying to force ourselves into a mold that was never designed for our neurology, we create space for a sense of self that is defined by authenticity rather than constant performance.

This journey toward sensory acceptance often involves a complex process of reframing our expectations of normalcy and success. For many, this looks like doing things differently in ways that might feel unconventional or even uncomfortable at first to those around us. It might involve changing how we work, how we socialize, or how we structure our domestic lives to minimize distress and prevent sensory spikes. While it is natural to feel a sense of loss or isolation when we cannot participate in the world in the same way as the majority, there is a profound and lasting peace to be found in prioritizing the stability of our own nervous system. By leaning into adaptability and practicing a deep level of self-compassion, we can build lives that respect our limitations while celebrating the unique and often vibrant ways in which we perceive the world. This shift in perspective allows us to move from a state of constant defense and survival to one of intentional, grounded, and meaningful living.

Understanding the sensory landscape of neurodivergence also requires us to acknowledge that our needs may fluctuate based on internal and external stressors. What is manageable one day may be overwhelming the next, and this variability is not a sign of inconsistency, but rather a reflection of a dynamic biological system. Embracing this reality allows us to let go of the rigid standards we often impose upon ourselves in an attempt to appear more typical. Instead of focusing on the frustration of what we cannot change, we can focus on the creative solutions that allow us to engage with the world on our own terms. This might mean advocating for sensory-friendly spaces, seeking out communities that understand these challenges, or simply giving ourselves permission to rest when the world becomes too much. Ultimately, the goal is to foster an environment where our sensory experiences are not seen as obstacles to be overcome, but rather as valid aspects of our identity that deserve space and respect.

What is Sensory Dysregulation?

Sensory diversity represents the unique ways in which individuals perceive the world through their senses, whereas sensory dysregulation refers to the states of distress that occur when one's sensory system is in upheaval. While a regulated nervous system operates in states of regulation or motivation, a dysregulated nervous system can move into meltdown, shutdown, fight-flight-freeze, or burnout.

While pioneers of sensory processing disorder and sensory integration dysfunction primarily focused on either sensory profiles or deficits, my preference is to simplify the language and move from a diagnostic framework to a more bottom-up inspired concept of our sensory worlds and how we perceive them. Emotional and sensory regulation are common concepts when we are discussing young children, especially those who must still co-regulate with a parental figure. Co-regulation refers to the state in which the nervous system of two individuals becomes synced together as a part of human development. This process is important for emotional, cognitive, and behavioural development. However, as children grow into teenagers, young adults, and adults, regulation moves from co-regulation to the area of self-regulation. Dr. Stuart Shanker of the MERHIT Centre provides a thorough overview of self-regulation in his book Self-Reg.

If co-regulation and self-regulation are the acts of becoming in-sync with our biological, emotional, and cognitive needs, then dysregulation is an appropriate term for an inability to regulate. With this in mind, I consider misophonia, misokinesia, and other sensory overloads to be within the realm of sensory dysregulation. Our brains and bodies are unable to sync together to process sensory experiences in a way that is seamless—and thus distress and a fight-flight-freeze response ensues. I think it is less about which senses are overstimulated—sound, sight, tactile, smell—and more about the act of being out-of-sync. While I am cognizant of different sensory profiles, such as sensory seekers, sensory avoiders, and more, there is enough discomfort and distress to single out sensory dysregulation. I admit that this term is imperfect, but it is my attempt to thread the needle between multidisciplinary approaches to development, cognition, and a bottom-up approach to the mind and body. For that purpose, sensory dysregulation refers to any sensory system that is functioning in an atypical manner or simply overloaded by stimuli. I am purposefully avoiding terms like Sensory Over-Responsivity due to its connection to Sensory Processing Disorder, as I am more concerned with sensory experiences in general than I am with a diagnostic explanation for how our sensory systems interact with the world around us.

Sensory Processing Disorder as it is proposed offers three subtypes which then each have more subtypes, including Sensory Modulation Disorder (which includes sensory over-responsivity, sensory under-responsivity, and sensory craving), Sensory-Based Motor Disorder (dyspraxia, postural disorder), and Sensory Discrimination Disorder (discrimination disorders and interoception). While these proposed terms show a variation in dysregulated sensory systems, the segmentation can be confusing for persons with sensory dysregulation as well as their parents and clinicians. As terms relating to sensory processing, there is great value in literature that can name specific parts of sensory dysregulation; however, I find it much easier to refer to the broader term sensory dysregulation as individuals with neurodivergence often have their own blends of categories that do not fit neatly into a category or sub-category.

Sensory profiles, on the other hand, are an arrangement of how persons with sensory dysregulation handle or seek sensory input. This conceptualization has four categories: sensory registration, sensory seeking, sensory sensitivity, and sensory avoiding; with all resting on a scale of high to low tolerance and passive and active response. While these terms are useful, many persons with sensory dysregulation cross thresholds and change needs contextually.

For the purpose of this book, I am using sensory dysregulation without dysfunction or disorder as I believe that there is much more to learn about how neurodivergent persons navigate the sensory world. In my view, whether we call it a *disorder* or *dysfunction* is less important than considering the experiences of persons with atypical sensory needs, and practical and evidence-based ways to help these individuals thrive within their own personal sensory landscape.

While this is not a prescriptive description of sensory-based experiences, it can be useful to consider different ways in which we process the world. While Sensory Integration Dysfunction and Sensory Processing Disorder aim to provide rigid definitions of sensory states, I do not prefer this language as real-world sensory experiences are more fluid and can be experienced by the same individual in a flux state.

Part of my conceptualization of sensory dysregulation in this book revolves around the sensory compass that I created as part of my clinical practice working with sensory dysregulation and my own sensory processing issues. In this view, there are six core states of sensory regulation and dysregulation that can be moved through at different times. These encompass the following: regulated, motivated, meltdown, fight-flight-freeze, burnout, and shutdown.

Sensory versus Emotional Regulation

Emotional regulation refers to a person's ability to regulate their emotional responses and control their behaviour and mood. Top-down approaches, such as CBT, DBT, and ACT, focus on changing emotional reactions and cognitive thoughts to better manage tolerance to heightened emotions. Sensory regulation, however, moves the emotional and cognitive part of regulation to the outer rings of regulation and first considers a bottom-up approach of the body and nervous system. For example, if a person feels distress and fear on a neurophysiological level, it is impossible to regulate the emotional response until the underlying physiological response is considered.

I developed the following Sensory and Emotion Regulation Compass to help neurodivergent individuals, their caregivers, and their educators and clinicians identify sensory states from the bottom to the top.

The Sensory and Emotion Regulation Compass

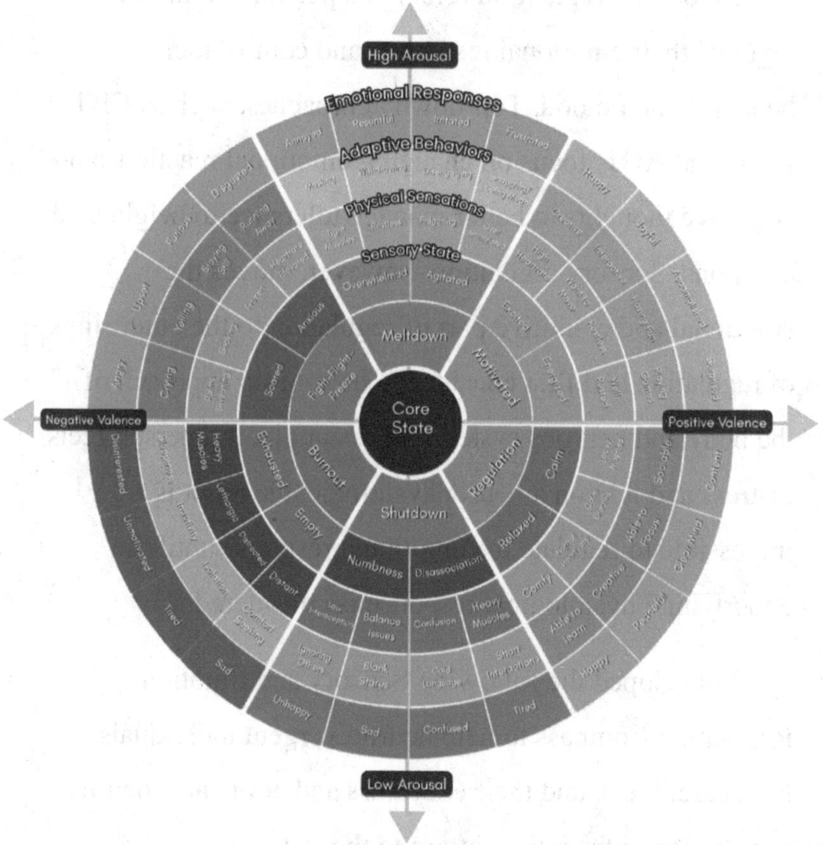

The sensory and emotion regulation compass is a clinical and self-help tool designed to help persons with neurodivergence and sensory dysregulation to identify their sensory states and coinciding physiological and emotional sensations and responses. The goal of the compass is not to give a rigid prescriptive description, but rather to provide a flexible tool. Many neurodivergent persons struggle with alexithymia, which is the inability to describe one's emotional states. The sensory compass is meant to help people navigate these complex physiological states and their emotional aftermath.

The sensory compass is meant to be navigated from the inner rings outwards and is presented from a bottom-up approach to sensory processing rather than a top-down approach. The bottom-up approach refers to physiological states happening before emotional processing, rather than the antiquated view that our thoughts and cognition cause our emotional states.

The compass is split into domains of negative and positive valence and high arousal and low arousal before moving through core states, sensory states, physical sensations, adaptive behaviours, and emotional responses. These states are explained in later sections.

Worksheet: Navigating the Sensory and Emotion Regulation Compass

Instructions: Use this worksheet when you are feeling dysregulated, recovering from overload, or checking in with your nervous system. Rather than starting with an emotional label, use the Compass to trace your experience from the inside out, starting with physical sensations and moving toward your core state and emotional needs.

Step 1: Body Check-In (Physical Sensations and Sensory States). Look at the inner rings of the Compass. What physical cues or sensory shifts do you notice in your body right now?

Examples: tight muscles, heavy limb feeling, racing heart, shallow breathing, buzzing, numbness, nausea, overstimulated, restless.

Step 2: Identify Your Core Nervous System State. Based on your physical cues and sensory environment, which core state best reflects where your nervous system is operating right now? Remember that states can overlap.

- Regulated
- Motivated
- Fight-Flight-Freeze
- Meltdown
- Shutdown
- Burnout

If overlapping, describe:

Step 3: Recognize Adaptive Behaviours and Urges
Look at the Adaptive Behaviours ring. How is your body responding to cope with, survive, or navigate this state?
Examples: masking, withdrawing, fidgeting, seeking movement, disengaging, snapping, seeking comfort, isolating.

Step 4: Name Emotional Responses
Now that you have checked in with your body and behaviour, what emotional feelings or interpretations are emerging on the outer ring?
Examples: anxious, frustrated, resentful, exhausted, overwhelmed, angry, peaceful, content, disconnected.

Step 5: Sensory Safety and Accommodation Needs
What does your nervous system need right now to feel safe, reduce demand, or support recovery?
Examples: noise-canceling headphones, entering a sensory-safe space, removing a sensory trigger, stepping away to rest, a weighted blanket, asking for an accommodation.

The Lost Tribe of Neurodivergence

As a person with sensory dysregulation and misophonia, I often find myself on the outskirts of neurodivergent advocacy. Despite so many overlapping attributes, I find myself at a loss when I have to explain sensory dysregulation and misophonia as there is currently no diagnosis or criteria. I have done countless screenings on myself for ADHD and Autism, and I never meet the criteria, even though my sensory scores are at the maximum end. Although I was 'diagnosed' with ADHD at seven years old, this has never felt like the true answer to my personal struggles. And yet, neurodivergence itself is the best way to explain my different brain and nervous system. I have found myself agreeing with many of the things I see in neurodivergent communities: different processing, cognitive overload, problems with understanding my body's internal states, the need for proprioceptive input, vestibular issues, and more. There is no formal description for those of us who suffer from numerous aspects of these neurodivergent states without a cut and dry diagnosis for autism or ADHD. This can lead to a feeling of not belonging anywhere. What I experience is not merely mental illness as my entire processing system is different from the 'neurotypical' experience, and yet, I do not have the language to explain my differences to those around me.

As a clinician, I know the power these labels can have for better or for worse. In the modern era, many people are organizing themselves through their identity and their lived and shared experiences. For those of us struggling with sensory dysregulation or neurodiverse brains that do not fit neatly in a box, this can be perplexing and confusing to navigate. While terms like Misophonia, Sensory Integration Dysfunction, and Sensory Processing Disorder exist, these are not verified diagnoses, and are rife with conflicts and inconsistencies—such as the conundrum of why persons with 'misophonia' often have other forms of dysregulation, such as sight, smell, and touch. SID and SPD are also debated heavily within their own communities, and thus this leaves us with more questions than answers.

This is why I use the term *sensory dysregulation,* because for those of us who are dysregulated without foundational language, we are often a lost tribe searching for answers. I do not think that a specific diagnosis is 100% necessary to explain our experiences, but I do believe we need shared language to help those who struggle to come together without tribes or pedantic arguments on exact definitions.

While I do not have ADHD or autism, I do identify as neurodivergent and I hope that shared language can help academics, advocates, and clinicians come together to understand forms of neurodivergence that live outside the previously existing criteria of diagnosis and help explain a more diverse neurological landscape.

Positive and Negative Valence

Sensory dysregulation creates a situation where there is high energy, such as fight-flight-freeze, and the autonomic nervous system is going haywire with the worry that there is a threat. In a situation where a person is triggered by misophonia, there is high arousal and negative valence; whereas in a situation where a person is excited and happy (such as during a dance party), their arousal is high, but their valence is positive.

There are situations where we can be upset and have negative valence and have low arousal—this is commonly called being "underresponsive" or "shutting down" in other conditions like sensory processing disorder/sensory integration or autism. It is useful to remember that our emotions and physiological reactions are more complex than just high arousal equals fight-flight-freeze. The reality of sensory dysregulation is that emotions are a complex biological, physiological, hormonal, and cognitive mixture.

Regulated and Motivated

The state of being regulated is often not discussed in sensory dysregulation on its own and is more often than not considered the default we are trying to achieve. However, it can be useful to define what sensory regulation is in itself. If sensory dysregulation is what happens when a person is *not* in a state of regulation, then regulation is by its nature the absence of fight-flight-freeze, shutdowns, meltdowns, and burnout. Being regulated does not necessarily mean being 'relaxed' or in a state of bliss, but is instead a baseline functioning where a neurodivergent person is able to perform daily functions. Motivation, similarly, is the absence of distress, but it also includes a positive valence and a boost of energy that is above a neutral baseline that builds upon basic regulation. Regulation is required for functioning and executive performance, whereas motivation takes this further and is a state of thriving. For example, a person reading a book and listening to music may be regulated, whereas a person who is playing an intense game of soccer or working on a creative piece of artwork is also motivated.

Fight-Flight-Freeze

Fight-flight-freeze is a nervous system state that is often most distressing for those with sensory dysregulation. Common terms for fight-flight-freeze from sensory stimuli are over-responsivity, misophonia, and misokinesia. These words all explain the same thing: a neurophysiological event where sensory stimuli causes an autonomic nervous system response. Misophonia refers specifically to 'hatred of sound' and has been represented in popular press and academic literature; similarly misokinesia means 'hatred of movement' where sensory over-responsivity is not exclusive to auditory or visual stimuli and incorporates bright lights, textures, scents, and all sensorial experiences. While much of my work has been on misophonia, for the sake of this book and sensory dysregulation as a concept, I prefer referring to fight-flight-freeze as a state of sensory dysregulation. I do not differentiate between types of sensory stimuli, and am instead discussing any sensory stimuli that causes a fight-flight-freeze response. However, for those who suffer extensively from misophonia or misokinesia, I suggest looking into my other works titled *Misophonia Matters* and *Cognitive behavioural Therapy (CBT) for Misophonia.*

When the brain and body enter fight-flight-freeze, there are only so many responses available to us as a reaction. We can either fight, flee, or completely freeze in response. For sensory dysregulation, fight rarely amounts to violence unless in young children, yet there might be thoughts of anger and disgust, or a verbal outburst asking the person to stop (perhaps unkindly). Flight is self-explanatory, since when facing sensory stimuli triggers, many with sensory dysregulation leave the environment if they can. Freeze tends to be more perplexing for those who are triggered and those around them. Freeze can amount to feeling unable to react or even staring at the triggering offender. Consider this, if you were in a room with a person you do not know who is wielding a knife in your direction—would you take your eyes off the knife?

The Autonomic Nervous System (ANS) is a complex part of the body that controls the fight-flight-freeze response, as well as other necessary functions for human existence.

The autonomic nervous system is a component of the peripheral nervous system that regulates involuntary physiologic processes including heart rate, blood pressure, respiration, digestion, and sexual arousal. It contains three anatomically distinct divisions: sympathetic, parasympathetic, and enteric. (Waxenbaum, 2023)

The autonomic nervous system (ANS) is made up of pathways of neurons that control various organ systems inside the body, using many diverse chemicals and signals to maintain homeostasis. It divides into the sympathetic and parasympathetic systems. The sympathetic component is better known as "fight or flight" and the parasympathetic component as "rest and digest." It functions without conscious control throughout the lifespan of an organism to control cardiac muscle, smooth muscle, and exocrine and endocrine glands, which in turn regulate blood pressure, urination, bowel movements, and thermoregulation. (LeBouef, 2023)

Fight-flight-freeze is our body's way of helping us identify and deal with threats, and for reasons we do not yet know, sensory dysregulation causes this release of adrenaline in the body which causes distress when faced with aversive sensory stimuli. Habituation refers to the state where a person becomes accustomed to a state or stimuli. For people with sensory dysregulation, habituation is a state that we never achieve as our nervous systems do not become accustomed to the triggering sounds or visuals.

Meltdowns and Shutdowns

Meltdowns and shutdowns are what happen when neurodivergent and sensory needs are not met. Meltdowns and shutdowns can occur together—with meltdowns coming before shutdowns, or on their own as nervous system responses. If meltdowns and shutdowns are recurring frequently and unmitigated, long-term impacts on the individual can lead to burnout, reduced mental health, and other complications. Reducing meltdowns and shutdowns is not about managing the behaviour of the individual, but rather about protecting them from the distress that accompanies these states.

Meltdowns and shutdowns look different on an individual basis, and some may mask these responses to appear as though they are in less distress. Masking, however, takes more energy and can lead to more long-term distress. Meltdowns are often characterized by being in fight-flight-freeze, being emotional, feeling like nothing is 'right', and discomfort in numerous senses. Shutdowns, however, are often a quieter form of distress where disassociation, numbness, and an inability to process stimuli are present. These are no perfected definitions of these states as an individual can experience some symptoms of meltdown and shutdown simultaneously. These terms are useful for helping caregivers, educators, and clinicians to understand nervous system states, but they are not prescriptive in nature, for rather they are descriptive and should be used in a way that serves the individual and not in a way that pathologizes their nervous system reactions. It is also important to understand that meltdowns and shutdowns are *not* a behavioural response, but rather they are a biological response.

Neurodivergent Burnout

Neurodivergent burnout refers to a state where a person who is neurodivergent experiences negative impacts from operating in a world that is not specifically designed for neurodivergent persons. The word *burnout* can lead to assumptions that this is referring to a state of being over-tired and simply needing rest, but neurodivergent burnout is much deeper than that.

Burnout has been shown consistently in literature on neurodivergent experiences such as Autism and ADHD. Burnout comes as a physical, psychological, and physiological response to masking, being exposed to sensory-based triggers, and to navigating spaces that are not designed for the neurodivergent mind and body. While the term burnout is also used in the neurotypical world to discuss extreme emotional states or an inability to perform due to increased stress or emotional fatigue, it should be noted that burnout for neurodivergent individuals can impact the entire nervous system.

Literature on burnout in neurodivergent populations has shown an increase risk of suicidal ideation and depression in individuals whose neurophysiological and sensory needs were systemically ignored, leading to the state of burnout. With this in mind, the price of burnout is much higher than simply being overwhelmed or exhausted.

Managing and avoiding burnout is more complex than simply ensuring self-care and check-ins. For neurodivergent individuals, balancing their needs is a daily struggle. For example, an overrun nervous system that has had to sit in a classroom for four hours with sensory dysregulating triggers such as pens clicking, legs shaking, and fluorescent lights, while simultaneously trying to pay attention and learn, is likely to come out of this situation depleted. It is not as simple as going home and taking a calming walk and drinking water. For a person with systemic dysregulation, there needs to be a plan in place before entering triggering situations, during the situation to lessen the dysregulation and provide accommodation of needs, and after the situation to provide neurophysiological and emotional support. A sensory regulation and accommodation plan are useful tools to assist in this process.

Sensory Craving

While overresponsivity is discussed frequently when it comes to sensory stimuli, underresponsivity and sensory craving are also important pieces of the puzzle. It should be noted that these are not mutually exclusive, and individuals with sensory dysregulation may have some overresponsive reactions, some underresponsive reactions, and a mix of both. There can also be variability on the same day. For example, while first awake and groggy, an individual may require extra stimuli like energetic music, cold drinks, and fresh air or bright sun. This same individual may become overwhelmed midday and require the exact opposite sensory environment to regulate their nervous system.

Many individuals may also need multiple stimuli to feel focused. Although this can seem counterintuitive to many, some neurodivergent persons focus better while multitasking. For example, I prefer to write, watch YouTube, and tab out to do marketing work at the same time. Neurotypical parents, teachers, and managers may see these behaviours as "not paying attention", but in reality these activities are like levers being pulled to get the exact right amount of sensory input to focus our attention on the task at hand. Attention and focus for neurodivergent individuals is not always linear, and should be considered normal functioning rather than something to adjust or 'fix'.

Masking or Camouflaging

Masking or camouflaging refers to a known aspect of neurodivergent life where individuals will hide their needs such as their cognitive fatigue, sensory overload, discomfort at touch or with eye-contact, and more. Neurodivergent individuals who mask may not seem like they need accommodations as they are spending a great deal of their energy and capabilities to maintain this façade. Unfortunately, for many neurodivergent individuals masking is a learned adaptive behaviour based on how the world has handled their needs in the past. While it is incredibly taxing to mask—even leading to meltdowns, shutdowns, and burnout—masking can still be the default adaptive behaviour due to traumatic past experiences, a lack of accommodations, and an unsupportive environment. While the impact of masking on the individual is significant, so is the conflict that can arise for neurodivergent individuals in situations where their needs are dismissed or even shamed.

For example, I know of persons with misophonia whose sensory dysregulation is triggered by loud sounds, yet who nonetheless refuse to wear headphones because they do not want to explain why they are 'different' or 'weird', especially in situations where these accommodations would otherwise be inappropriate, such as a classroom where only the individual with accommodations would be wearing headphones. Dealing with masking is not just about changing the perspective for the neurodivergent individual, but also about changing the narratives and public perception of all persons to foster understanding and acceptance of neurodivergent accommodation needs.

Sensory Safety

For persons with sensory dysregulation, safety is hard to come by. When I talk about safety in this way, I am not talking about just the basics—like shelter, food, and water—I am talking about the nervous system's ability to regulate and become calm. Our bodies are not able to regulate if we are unable to feel safe. Often with clients with sensory dysregulation I pose the following question: if you were in a room with a poisonous snake, would you be able to feel safe? Would trying to think the snake away work? The answers are usually, no, and no.

Safety cannot happen by sheer willpower alone; it takes environmental changes and accommodations to help the individual with sensory dysregulation. This is not focusing on *adapting* in the sense of getting used to the environment or masking until there is burnout. Safety is an imperative part of coping with sensory dysregulation and should be paramount for helping individuals who are mismatched with their environments. While safety is not *always attainable,* especially in situations like public transportation, clinics, etc., this merely underlines the importance of having a safe home environment even more. Persons with sensory dysregulation are constantly in environments that do not meet their needs, so safety must be cultivated and maintained.

Creating a Safe Space

Whether the person with sensory dysregulation is a child, a teenager, or an adult, having a safe space in their home to calm down is an integral part of coping with sensory dysregulation. Since sensory dysregulation involves being dysregulated with a state of panic and fear, safety is an important means of managing this overload. This safe space can be as small as a closet, or as large as an entire room. This is of course dependent on the space available to the person with sensory dysregulation. If there are no spaces in the home available, such as with a roommate in a shared living situation, one potential accommodation is a bed tent. Bed tents are set up over your bed, with your mattress inside, creating a safe and private space without taking up extra room in the home.

As much as reasonably possible, the safe space should be quiet or with pleasant sounds, lit in a way that is amenable to the sufferer, and be generally soothing to the person it is designed for. In an otherwise loud space, a noise generator or fan can be used to drown out sounds. The use of headphones, earplugs, and music can also be helpful to enhance the space.

With traditional sensory diets in mind, this safe space can be filled with activities, scents, and materials that the person finds calming. For example, within this room we could find painting supplies, a white noise machine, a diffuser for essential oils, teddy bears to hug, and dimmable lights. This experience will be different for each person and will of course vary based on the layout of a home. This sensory space could even be a living room or a bedroom if you plan for it accordingly. The idea is to have a set space to calm down when overstimulated.

The following is a non-exhaustive list of things that could be present in a sensory-safe space:

- Sensory toys such as chewable necklaces or fidget toys.
- A scent diffuser or candle.
- Colouring books, art supplies, and other craft supplies.
- Books to read.
- Stuffed animals or comfy pillows to hug.
- Galaxy lamps (these are lamps that turn the ceiling into a starry night).
- A weighted blanket.
- Playdough, kinetic sand, or slime.

The idea of this sensory space is that it is a calming retreat from an otherwise busy and overwhelming world. This does not have to be a formalized space necessarily, but it is about choosing activities and environmental factors that are calming rather than overstimulating. For this reason, I did not suggest using television since this could be overstimulating with both visuals and sounds. However, some people may find classic TV shows, Disney movies, or even horror movies to be calming—and if that is the case, then go for it!

Worksheet: Planning Your Sensory Space

Instructions: Answer the following questions on how you will set up your sensory space and when you will utilize it.

Where is your sensory space?

What items do you already have that you can add to your sensory space?

What changes could you make to your sensory space to make it calmer?

When will you come to your sensory space?

Worksheet: Scheduling Your Coping Skills

Instructions: Plan and schedule specific times throughout your week to practice your coping skills.

Time	Monday	Tuesday	Wednesday	Thursday	Friday
7am					
8am					
9am					
10am					
11pm					
12pm					
1pm					
2pm					
3pm					
4pm					
5pm					
6pm					
7pm					
8pm					
9pm					
10pm					

Worksheet: Picking Activities You Enjoy

Instructions: List activities you enjoy that can serve as positive distractions or self-soothing techniques when dealing with sensory dysregulation. These are just ideas, feel free to add your own!

Circle or put a check mark next to the activities which helped you feel calm or in a better mood in the past.

Meditation

Swimming

Swinging

Golfing

Basketball

Walking

Reading

Playing a game

Yoga

Baseball

Crafting hobbies

Lifting weights

Sensory Regulation Activities

Based on the work of Susan Nesbit, M.S., OT, the following are considerations for dealing with sensory overload, sensory craving, shutdowns, and the need for consistent sensory input to regulate one's nervous system. This list is not exhaustive, but offers suggestions based on occupational therapy and sensory regulation.

Calming Activities
If you are over-stimulated, the following activities may help to calm you.

- Hugging/bear hugging with a partner.
- Tightly wrapping your arms around your torso and/or crossing your legs and/or squeezing your hands together.
- Cuddling with a partner or pets.
- Pushing against a wall as if to move it.
- Leaning forward with hands on edge of desk or table – gently pushing as if to move it; doing pushups if table is stable.
- Rolling up tightly in a blanket.
- Slow rocking, e.g., in a rocking chair.
- Swinging with slow, linear, and rhythmical movements.
- Walking/strolling in a park.
- Swimming laps.
- Carrying a laundry basket.
- Washing windows, mirrors, or tables.
- Pushing and pulling heavy items.
- Listening to rain, a waterfall, or ocean waves.

- Listening to a tabletop fountain or an aquarium.
- Listening to coloured noise.
- Taking a warm bath or shower, then rolling up in a large towel.
- Using calming scents such as lavender and/or rose in oils, soaps, lotions, or candles.
- Wearing compression clothing, e.g., short-sleeved and long-sleeved t-shirts, shorts, and pants.

Energizing Activities

If you need to be aroused, wake up your senses by trying some of these activities:

- Tug-of-War (pull on TheraBand tied around the doorknob of a closed door; use the strongest resistance possible).
- Pulling heavy items, e.g., suitcase or backpack on wheels.
- Jumping jacks/star jumps on the floor.
- Jumping on a mini-trampoline (use a backyard trampoline if one is available).
- Jumping rope.
- Bouncing on a hopper ball, exercise ball, or therapy ball (these balls come in adult sizes).
- Brisk/vigorous walking and race walking.
- Hiking uphill.
- Stair climbing: Race up the stairs, then go up the stairs two at a time (to cool off, walk at a normal pace down the stairs).
- Aerobics, including chair aerobics.
- Tumbling, e.g., cartwheels.
- Swimming: Doing flips and somersaults in the water.
- Spinning in rotating chair or on swing suspended from one hook.

- Using playground swings or a merry-go-round (you are never too old).
- Taking a cool shower.
- Using alerting scents such as citrus, mint, and/or pine in oils, soaps, lotions, or candles.

Organizing Activities

These activities may calm or energize, depending on your needs. Pay attention to your body for signs that indicate your level of arousal.

- Squeezing stress balls.
- Sucking, e.g., water from a squeeze bottle, a popsicle, or a lifesaver.
- Sucking drinkable (liquid) yogurt through a straw.
- Eating healthy, crunchy foods like carrots or chewy foods like jellybeans.
- Chewing bubble gum.
- Blowing soap bubbles.
- Climbing stairs (up and down) or a ladder.
- Doing pushups.
- Doing sit-ups.
- Doing jumping jacks.
- Tumbling and gymnastics.
- Doing headstands or handstands against a wall.
- Hiking, walking, or running.
- Roller skating, roller blading, or ice skating.
- Jumping rope.
- Biking/cycling.
- Stretching, including tai chi and yoga.
- Lying on your stomach to read a book.
- Pulling heavy items, e.g., a wagon filled with children, books, or laundry detergent.

- Colouring mandalas – begin at the center and work your way to the outside border.
- Sewing, knitting, crocheting, and weaving.

Neurodivergence and Identity

For many with neurodivergence, their identity is wrapped up tightly in their experiences. This can be seen in the prevalence of autistics who prefer identity-first language such as "autistics" rather than "persons with autism". This can be different across persons and neurodivergent experiences, which shows that identity is an important part of the equation—regardless of the preferences. Clinicians, educators, and partners should not assume the preferred way to refer to a neurodivergent person and should instead ask "Do you prefer ADHDer or person with ADHD?" which is a simple question that can alleviate tension and miscommunication.

It can be easy for clinicians to slip into patterns of saying "you are not your autism/adhd/ocd/etc.", but this is not always a *helpful* way to treat individuals who are living the experiences associated with neurodivergence. Identity is increasingly seen in literature as an important part of understanding one's neurodivergence and should not be pigeonholed into a neurotypical or rigid view. While it may be hard for a parent or clinician to understand *why* the identity 'autistic' or 'adher' are important—this is still the preference of many. Changing descriptions and person-centered language can be distressing to those who have built their identity surrounding their neurotypes. There is no right or wrong answer for describing one's neurotype other than by aligning with the person who is describing their own personal story.

Beyond Behaviour

Behaviour-based care for persons with neurodivergence happens under the auspices of different professionals, with CBT being a behaviour-based therapy that includes exposure therapy in some cases, but more insidiously through ABA, or Applied Behaviour Analysis which is frequently applied by teams. Unlike those who practice CBT, a form of psychotherapy, those who practice ABA are often untrained without proper credentials. Many ABA facilities operate with licensed individuals who are then monitoring several individuals below them. Training for these positions is often lacking, and the evidence that ABA works is flawed at best. While I have my own problems with behaviour therapy in general, even when it includes CBT and the use of behaviour and experiments to try and change neurophysiological realities and processing differences in the individual, ABA goes beyond this with their strict adherence to client "compliance".

Numerous children, adolescents, and adults have been traumatized by the use of ABA on neurodivergent individuals. This is more than an inappropriate treatment; it is a systemic failure of society to protect the vulnerable from pseudoscience cloaked as "treatment". Despite the growing evidence that ABA is cruel and causes negative outcomes for individuals, it continues to be used to try and "fix deficits" of neurodivergent persons. To put it bluntly, ABA's goal is to force compliance, masking, and inevitably prescribes burn-out as its mandate. The longer you last before you burnout in an ABA program, the more "compliant" you are.

CBT and other behavioural therapies are *less* concerning as they can be adapted appropriately for neurodivergent populations—this was my main goal of *Cognitive Behavioural Therapy (CBT) for Misophonia*, a book I wrote to re-write CBT to omit exposure therapy and deal instead with the emotional and relational aspects of misophonia outside of the neurophysiological response. With that said, there are still practitioners who misuse behavioural therapies with their neurodivergent clients, including a graded exposure therapy approach or a "strengths-based" approach that tries to force the practitioner's or society's views on the client rather than reflecting the patient's worldviews and emotional and sensory-based needs.

Behaviour is not the full picture when it comes to how persons interact with the world. Instead, how we behave is a mix of our sensory and neurophysiological needs, our ways of processing information and stimuli, and our own values and ideals. What one person may view as a "negative behaviour", such as withdrawing from friends and spending time reading alone, another person may uphold as their necessary peace and solitude. The problem with therapies based on behaviours is that there is some idyllic behaviour that is considered *correct*. Where we get these values is often from neurotypical assumptions, learned prejudices, and our own biases.

While I am not saying that all behaviours related to neurodivergence are positive, I am saying that we must consider the bottom-up approach to regulation before we can seriously consider helping an individual adapt and interact with their environment in a way that is positive for the individual and those around them, without changing the individual to fit a mold. With that said, there are times such as when a neurodivergent individual is hitting, screaming, or lashing out and these behaviours can lead to dysregulation or a lack of safety in the overall environment. This should of course be mediated, but it should not be handled in a purely punitive way, as communication skills, sensory regulation, and adult-caregiver guided mediation can help with these ruptures in relationships.

I am by no means saying that issues of behaviour do not exist, but I am saying that behaviour is much more complex than an individual simply choosing a way of acting based on a preformulated thought. Behaviours are the accumulation of our nervous systems, physical environments, and emotional states. If we try to change behaviour with compliance alone, we miss far too many factors of personhood to lead to meaningful change.

Accessibility in Design

Every day we navigate our lives through design and architectural decisions made by somebody else. Whether we are discussing physical architecture and design or software, hardware, and UI/UX (user interface/user experience) design, every choice made by the creators has an impact on the users trying to interact with these systems. Part of my advocacy for vestibular and sensory over-responsivity has been focused on better design in the digital space.

We are not just talking about games or software that are optional—in today's world many of the devices and programs we interact with are now mandatory. For example, Microsoft Word and the office suite, Google and Android devices, iPhones, and more. I am specifically mentioning these products as I have been advocating for better accessibility with these companies for the past several years. If not for advocacy, I would not currently be able to write this book on my MacBook Air because the Microsoft Office suite previously had a blinking text cursor caret (|) that made me dizzy and sick whenever I tried to write. Similarly, the iPhone and MacBook have added options for "prefers cursor non-blink". While not every device has changed as of yet for this feature, my life has significantly improved with headaches declining and productivity increased as my vestibular system is no longer under assault as I interact with necessary devices and programs.

Accessibility is not limited to the physical world around us, although there are certainly still strides to be made for physical disabilities, wheelchair access, and functional building and city design that help those who have these physical needs. With that said, the ability to use hardware and software is often limited to things such as *colour blindness, text size, reduced motion that does not reduce motion in most cases, and screen readers.* I am not against any of these accessibility features, but rather I believe there is much room for improvement and believe that designers need to be thinking more critically than just ADA checkboxes for a truly accessible experience.

Planning Sensory Activities for Sensory States

Choose sensory activities that may help you when you are in the following sensory states. Remember that these are suggestions and that you do not have to do them every time—instead these should be ideas for you to turn to in the moment. Choose multiple options for each state so that you have a list of suggestions ready in the moment. Regulated and motivated are not included as these suggestions are meant for going back to a state of regulation or motivation.

My sensory activities for burnout…

My sensory activities for meltdowns…

My sensory activities for fight-flight-freeze…

My sensory activities for shutdowns…

Executive Dysfunction

It should be of no surprise that persons who experience sensory dysregulation, cognitive and processing challenges, and neurophysiological experiences in a way that diverges from those who are neurotypical will often have challenges 'getting things done' or 'sticking to a schedule'. We often call these executive functioning skills—the ability to run one's life in a way that is meeting our needs or the expectations put upon us. I want to make a note that in some cases executive dysfunction is something that the individual may be distressed by and want to work on adapting these skills—but there are also "dysfunction" cases where it is the parents, teachers, co-workers, or bosses who are trying to impose a standard on a neurodivergent individual that is unfair to their nervous system and their own processing needs.

Common concerns that fall under 'executive functioning' are things such as personal hygiene, time management, chores like groceries, laundry, cleaning, cooking, paying bills, meeting deadlines, attending meetings, and more. In some cases these needs are necessary for life such as drinking water and eating. However, it should be noted that many neurodivergent individuals choose accommodations to help them through these functioning experiences and that should be validated rather than shamed. For example, a neurodivergent individual may choose to eat microwave dinners, use disposable cutlery, and even have a sponge bath when a full shower or bath is too overwhelming. Executive functioning is never as simple as not being able to complete an activity, as there are always nuances such as sensory needs and dysregulation, cognitive overload if too much is on one's mind, emotional dysregulation such as when struggling mentally, and numerous other factors. The following exercise titled Neurotypical Expectation versus Accommodation focuses on neurotypical expectations such as using regular cutlery or reusable water bottles versus using plastic and paper or single-use water bottles. This exercise aims to normalize and destigmatize executive dysfunction choices for those with sensory dysregulation.

Neurotypical Expectation versus Accommodation

Neurotypical Expectation	**Accommodation**

When Calming Doesn't Calm

Often neurodivergent persons are given standard anxiety advice when they are feeling fight-flight-freeze, meltdowns, shutdowns, or burnout. The problem with these "self-care" suggestions for managing anxiety and promoting calmness is that our nervous systems are dysregulated beyond the point that basic intervention can mitigate. This can be further complicated if the neurodivergent person faces somatic anxiety experiences with breathing exercises, discomfort with meditation tracks, or an inability to focus or clear one's mind when dealing with executive dysfunction, cognitive load, or sensory dysregulation.

Pastimes that relax some individuals may be overly taxing for neurodivergent persons, including things as simple as watching videos, an evening walk, or reading a book. Depending on current needs, an activity that was enjoyable or relaxing before may also become overstimulating in a different circumstance. This can be hard to explain as the variability of coping capabilities is a wide spectrum. Depending on the scope of sensory and cognitive needs that day, the brain and body's ability to regulate can vary widely from moment to moment, let alone from day to day.

The physical characteristics of a room, the presence of others, the presence of stimuli or food, the type of activity, and more can impact the tolerance of an activity. For example, I personally find watching television in my living room to be a highly stimulating activity, while my husband and my father both consider this to be a time to relax. In the living room, there is often snacking with the television, if it is daytime bright light from the patio door, the sound of neighbours out the window, and the sound of a dog and music through a shared townhouse wall. However, I do watch television in my bedroom on my second monitor while I am working or playing video games. To some, this may sound overstimulating since there are multiple things going on at once, but for me there are differences that make this more sensory friendly. In my bedroom, I control the lighting exactly, I have curtains that block the sun, I have white noise playing constantly, and my room is one of the only rooms in the house that does not share a single wall with a neighbor. I also frequently watch shows I have already seen, especially comforting things like Disney movies or low-effort content like YouTube. This makes it much easier to handle.

The ability to regulate one's senses and emotions is not always cut and dry. There are many differences that can influence whether or not something is calming or dysregulating. When I am already overstimulated to the point of meltdown and shutdown, I am unable to play video games or watch television and normally at this point the only things that work are painting my nails, blasting white noise, taking a bath, or going to bed. My needs are specific to my nervous system and environment, and each neurodivergent person has their own specific and individualized needs.

Freedom to Choose

A common concept in neurodivergent advocacy and literature is Pervasive Drive for Autonomy, which was previously known as Pathological Demand Avoidance. The term was changed by the community itself to remove harmful behavioural associations with the biological need for freedom and autonomy. Work on PDA first came from the view that persons with neurodivergence were avoiding the demands of others such as in education or home settings. For a child who was deemed to have PDA, a typical behaviour may be rejecting cleaning their room, refusing to stop playing with toys when there are other things to do, or even destructive activities like breaking things or yelling.

Rather than acknowledge an underlying sensory or physiological need, these behaviour-based practitioners would attempt punishments or rewards (i.e. If you do not stop that you will not get to play your game; if you do stop, you can have 30 minutes of play time). The move to redefine PDA as pervasive drive for autonomy aims to fill in this gap and acknowledge that rather than misbehaving or 'acting out', these neurodivergent children, teens, and even adults are desperate for their own sense of self and autonomy.

Both of these terms are oversimplying in my opinion, and while I do believe pervasive drive for autonomy is much better than pathological demand avoidance, I do believe both are missing the mark. Rather than a *pervasive drive*, persons with neurodivergence are normal human beings who would like to continue existing in a way that serves their own brain and body.

If a 'behaviour' is something that needs to be adjusted—i.e. Stop hitting somebody, stop breaking a toy, spend time doing something else—then these needs can be communicated in a way that is not pathologizing. For example, when we take an example of a mother telling her young child to stop playing with his toys and clean his room, this neurotypical child may commonly reply to this request by questioning the need to change activities by saying "why?" or "I do not want to." In many cases, parents will choose to say something along the lines of "because I said so" and this rarely works in their favour.

Just like the neurotypical child, the neurodivergent child is not misbehaving or acting out, but rather they are feeling a mismatch in their personal wants and needs and that of those around them. Rather than treat the neurodivergent individual as 'bad' or 'non-compliant', it is far more respectful, neuroaffirming, and effective to explain *why* this behaviour must stop and let the neurodivergent individual have a say in how they will. For example, in response to "go clean your room now", the neurodivergent child may say "I understand I need to clean my room, but I would like to have a snack first as I am hungry." This leaves room for accommodation and autonomy while also mitigating the impact of the behaviour.

Neurodivergent Shame

Neurodivergent apologizing and shame are something I have seen in my clinical practice, but also in my own life. It can be hard to reconcile one's inabilities or challenges and rather than accepting that we are different from others, these differences can sometimes be perceived as inadequacies or failures. This is further perpetuated when behavioural interventions, rigid neurotypical values, or unfair comparisons are used.

It can be easy to say that neurodivergent persons should not feel shame for their neurotypes and their mind and body operating in a way that is not 'neurotypical', but in reality we are often faced with pushback at both micro and macro levels—this can be as simple as somebody asking why you are not 'paying attention' if you use a fidget tool, or as macro as being told that you cannot do a job due to being autistic.

Mitigating shame is both an act of advocacy, wherein the world around us learns to adapt and accept neurodivergent functioning, but also an act of self-compassion. Neither of these are easy, and both are required to finally dissolve the unnecessary burden of shame for persons who are neurodivergent. It is imperative for parents, clinicians, educators, and neurodivergent persons to understand that shame is not a personal failure, nor is an inability to conform to a rigid standard that does not align with one's brain and body—shame, rather, is something that is an imposition on one's character, and whether externalized or internalized, it should be mitigated to help persons who are neurodivergent to flourish.

Being Neurodivergent in School and Work

For many with sensory dysregulation, school or work can become extremely challenging, and sometimes even impossible. Behavioural approaches refer to the act of a child or teen not going to school as "school refusal" and often frame this as a personal behavioural failure rather than an institutional failure to accommodate the needs of neurodivergent children.

Rather than focus on helping individuals with neurodivergence cope at school or work—it is often put on the individual to comply and twist themselves into something that is more palpable for the institutions. While there have been strides for accommodations for disabilities, such as working from home, days off, sensory spaces in schools, using headphones and more, this does not mean that accommodations are being applied across the board and it also does not stop systemic barriers. For one thing, a neurodivergent person may not even be considered for a job in a field that they are trained in if those hiring are strict about working in office rather than from home. This is a systemic issue that harms the person with neurodivergence regardless of their capability to do the job.

I have mentioned work and school in the same section because school is often our first step into institutional frameworks that do not serve our neurotypes and nervous systems. Often, school is the first experience an individual has with their needs not being met. Even when needs *are met* they are often hard fought and require bureaucracy, doctor's notes, and parental advocacy to even receive support necessary for growth and development.

Similarly, as neurodivergent persons enter post-secondary education and the workforce, laws exist for disabled persons, but they are not one-size-fits-all, nor are they automatically in place without a great deal of self-advocacy, systemic policies, and laws. Many are left behind while waiting for these systems to be put in place and in some cases, the accessibility barrier is so high that these individuals never make it through the door to even ask. For those who are 'fortunate' enough to receive accommodations, this does not mean there will not be pushback, with teachers, support workers, managers, and employers often pushing back and having their own unsolicited opinion on what *should* and *should not* be accommodated.

Milestones

Frequently I am asked if neurodivergent children will grow up to complete college or university, if they will find romantic partners, or live on their own. I almost always respond in the same way: if your child *wants to*. Now, this will obviously depend upon the specific needs of the individual, but I see no reason to place these fears on young neurodivergent children. As a personal anecdote, I am married and a therapist and have numerous sensory triggers that make everyday life challenging.

It is my view that considering the potential milestones of neurodivergent children and teenagers says more about the parents and community around them than it does for the neurodivergent individual. I still remember being a 16-year-old in my guidance counsellor's office being told I would "never go to college" because I was in the lower division of math. These assumptions were painful and heartbreaking at 16, but they were also wholly untrue. I now hold an honours diploma in Creative Digital Media, a Bachelor of Arts in Political Science, and a Master of Arts in Counselling Psychology with plans to continue my education.

Rather than finish traditional university for my bachelor's and master's, I finished these degrees through online schooling and utilized several programs for accommodation and support. The road was not easy even with this scaffolding, but it was possible. My bachelor's degree took me roughly seven years to complete rather than the traditional four, and yet I did finish.

My point with this personal story is that milestones for neurodivergent persons should be based on the needs and beliefs of the individual and not presumptions based on labels and functioning ability. I also push back against narratives that champion neurodivergence as a superpower that leads to exceptional outcomes—this also puts pressure on individuals that is nonsensical. The truth is that neurodivergent individuals are just that, individuals. The milestones one achieves in one's life are up to the individual to curate and work toward. For some, a milestone is the ability to go out and sit on a public bench on a crowded day, for another, a milestone may be finishing a degree. Neither is insignificant.

Protective Withholding

Protective withholding is not just a term for neurodivergent persons, it is also used for persons with trauma, mental disorders, and personality disorders. The concept of protective withholding refers to saving parts of yourself, your emotions, or your experiences that you are worried will be used against you or misunderstood by others.

Protective withholding is often a learned adaptive behaviour for persons whose needs have not been met in the past or whose interests or emotions have been used against them. This can be something as simple as being mocked for liking a certain TV show, or as complex as being told that their worldview is "wrong" or "silly". Protective withholding has less to do with the exact belief, idea, mood, or thought that is being protected and more to do with the fear of the repercussions of losing safety. The purpose of this chapter is to explain why persons with neurodivergence may not want to share things with others—even if that experience seems like it would be overwhelmingly positive for others. For example, sharing interests, games, skills, emotional moments and more, are often considered the peak of human interaction, yet for somebody who experiences protective withholding, it may be much harder to share these things in case it backfires.

Protective withholding is something that should be considered from the perspective of the individual experiencing it, and boundaries surrounding what neurodivergent individuals should share should come from the individual and not their parents, partners, friends, co-workers, or others around them. It can be hard to understand the need to withhold for protection, but this need is deeply personal and must be handled with care even by mental health professionals. If the individual sees their protective withholding, or some instances of it, as a thing to be changed, then this can be worked on in a way that is comfortable for that individual.

Forcing an individual, regardless of their sensory systems, neurodivergence, or mental conditions, to conform and share parts of themselves that they are not comfortable with can lead to the exact conditions that lead to protective withholding in the first place—a lack of understanding and safety in their relationships.

Taking Things Literally

Sarcasm and nuance are often considered neurotypical hallmarks of active listening and comprehension. However, these assumptions cannot be translated to all individuals, particularly many neurodivergent individuals. In many cases, individuals with neurodivergence may prefer conversations to be factual, blunt, and devoid of double meaning. Rather than a lack of intelligence, this is simply a more direct way of processing information. Communication patterns should not be considered behavioural issues, but rather, should be understood as different processing types. Not all neurodivergent individuals are direct or blunt, but many are.

Rigid expectations of communication can lead to unnecessary friction. For example, individuals who ask follow-up questions and directly ask "what do you mean?" when faced with a comment or question may be considered rude, despite no ill intent. By honouring communication styles and understanding that these differences are based on processing, not just social expectations and morality, we can help individuals communicate with one another without pre-conceived assumptions. Different does not mean wrong, and in-fact, this diversity of communication can lead to outcomes that are enriched by the different points of view and processing patterns of the world.

Gatekeeping

For neurodivergent individuals, sharing their interests, hobbies, and pieces of identity are often overwhelming, and even unbearable. While shared interests are considered to be an important part of relationship development by many neurotypical persons, this does not necessarily translate to some neurodivergent individuals. Gatekeeping refers to the act of keeping things that are special to oneself internally and engaging with their interests on their own terms and time, often without any hobby groups or friends and family sharing the activity.

Some neurodivergent individuals feel as though their interests are taken from them if another begins engaging with it to 'befriend' or 'connect' with them. Rather than an experience that grows bonds, this can be seen as a betrayal or an upsetting experience. Gatekeeping can also be wider than just in personal spheres—for example, not following tags, websites, or search engine results for a topic that one considers to be "theirs". I often experience this myself when it comes to literature, television, and topics that I frequently write about. This does not mean that the neurodivergent person never wishes to share their gatekept interest, but rather that any sharing is done from a place of comfort and ownership, not an experience to be taken or monopolized by the other person.

Unlike protective withholding, gatekeeping does not necessarily come from a place of trauma or disappointment. Rather, gatekeeping is about protecting and preserving important parts of one's identity without compromising or sharing these experiences entirely with others. Neurotypical responses to gatekeeping often focus on the idea that "no one owns x topic" and "shared interests are important". These views are largely unhelpful as they do not consider the differences in how a neurodivergent person may experience their interests and process them. Rather than being considered *incorrect* or *selfish* for this gatekeeping behaviour, it is important for neurotypical persons to understand that some interests are simply boundaries for the person with neurodivergence, and not something they want to share.

Grief

Being neurodivergent can lead to grief in many ways. Not all persons with neurodivergence and sensory challenges have always struggled in the same capacity. For example, some individuals have little to no challenges until they go to school or begin working in a field that causes problems. For others, sensory dysregulation can get worse over time or even appear much later in life. This, along with missing a life that one wishes they could have, can often lead to grief.

The grief that happens with neurodivergence is similar to the grief that happens when getting sick, losing a part of yourself, or having the world treat you in ways that are not congruent with your own values, beliefs, or how you wish your life to be. Just as a person with mobility loss may grieve their inability to climb stairs, a person with neurodivergence may grieve their inability to participate in events such as crowded parties, or their inability to make decisions based on whims rather than balancing sensory and neurophysiological needs on a tight rope.

Like all grief, neurodivergent grief is complex and highly individual. Some may have ongoing grief, others may feel it in moments where they are struggling, and others may not grieve at all. Clinicians, educators, and parents must understand that grief is highly individual and should not be defined for the individual. It is important to note that parents may have their own grief over their child's abilities and struggles which should be kept out of the equation when helping a neurodivergent person process their own feelings about their world and how they manage it.

Why Does Advocacy Matter?

In a busy world, it can be daunting to imagine dedicating your time through volunteering or spreading awareness of sensory dysregulation. With that said, advocating for yourself, your loved ones, and others around you, is one of the most important ways that we can change the world. Advocacy does not have to be flashy campaigns or full-time dedication. Educating others and highlighting resources is an important part of advocacy. Fighting for your own accommodations or those of your client is a means of advocacy that not only helps an individual, but also the greater population as these accommodations become more widespread and accepted. Advocacy is a series of actions, and over time, even the smallest of these actions add up to meaningful change.

Advocacy can help us change the world around us and is powerful in the everyday lives of persons with sensory dysregulation. For example, through advocacy we can help teachers, doctors, and even researchers understand the needs of the sensory community and thus help guide the narrative that leads to better accommodations, research, and acceptance of persons with sensory dysregulation and sensory disorders.

Self-advocacy is the process in which persons with sensory dysregulation learn to explain sensory dysregulation to others, negotiate accommodations, and become aware of their boundaries when it comes to triggering environments. Some persons with sensory dysregulation worry that asking for accommodations will be met with resistance or even think that they should not ask for accommodations at all because it is “their problem”. It is my belief that this is not true and that persons with sensory dysregulation deserve to live enriched lives without being constantly dysregulated.

Script for Explaining Sensory Dysregulation

The goal of explaining sensory dysregulation is to help people understand that your reactions are a real, involuntary physiological response, not an emotional choice or a personal dislike. By focusing on how your nervous system processes sensory information, you remove blame and build genuine understanding.

Script: "Hey, I wanted to share something about how my brain and body work. I experience sensory dysregulation. When I am exposed to certain sights, sounds, or textures—like [stimuli here]—my autonomic nervous system misinterprets those inputs as a physical threat, triggering a sudden fight-flight-freeze reaction. It is not a dislike or a choice; it is a physiological response that causes real distress. I am telling you this so you know what is happening if I ever need to step away or adjust my environment."

Write Your Own Script

Script for Asking Strangers to Accommodate

The key to this exercise is to be polite and not put blame on the offending trigger. By asking for help and staying neutral when asking for accommodations, you are much less likely to anger the recipient of the request. In a perfect world, accommodations would be far easier to ask for, but in the world we live in it is important to mitigate frustration when explaining the disorder.

Sample Script

Script: Hello, excuse me I am so sorry to ask you this, but would you mind not doing [stimuli here], I experience sensory dysregulation and it causes me distress. I would really appreciate it if you would be willing to help me.

Write your own script

Advocacy and Accommodation

Advocacy and accommodation are paramount for coping with sensory dysregulation and accompanying challenges. For persons with sensory dysregulation, much of the world is not set up to handle our basic needs. For example, classrooms, work areas, and more are based on the needs of neurotypical populations and challenges with socializing, working, learning, and even the home environment can arise. For a person with sensory dysregulation, the safety that comes for neurotypical individuals in spaces may never come—the lights may be too bright, their clothes too tight, the room paradoxically too silent with every noise too loud, and more.

Advocacy can refer to self-advocacy, parent or clinician advocacy, or community advocacy. Each of these is important for improving the daily lives of individuals with neurodivergence. Self-advocacy can be as simple as asking to move tables in a workplace environment to as complex as working on changing institutional policies. Advocacy should be up to the individual to decide their level of comfort. While accommodation and self-advocacy are important parts of functioning in a world that is not set up for one's nervous system, it is also not the job of the neurodivergent person to be constantly educating those around them. This is where community advocacy from clinicians, advocates, and institutional designers must step in to bridge these gaps. Accommodation requirements are also hard-fought by advocates and clinicians, and advocacy is the key pillar to improving the lives of neurodivergent people by promoting policies and standards of care that are neuroaffirming and help challenge traditional narratives on the 'correct' way to interact with school, work, and society.

The following accommodation plan draft can be used by clinicians and modified.

Sample Accommodation Letter

The following accommodation letter is provided as a sample for clinicians, or for parents or neurodivergent persons to bring to their own clinicians as an idea. This letter must not be reproduced directly.

Sample Accommodation Letter

To Whom It May Concern,

My name is [Clinician Name] and I am a [License/Scope Here]. I have worked with [Client Name] over the past [timeframe, e.g., year] in a psychotherapeutic capacity. This letter is intended to provide clinical observations and summarize the therapeutic focus of treatment within my scope as a [Clinician Role]. It should not be interpreted as a formal diagnostic, custody, or forensic assessment.

Over the course of our clinical relationship, therapeutic work has focused on the following:

- sensory regulation and sensory dysregulation-related distress,
- emotional regulation,
- autistic overload and burnout,
- coping strategies for sensory sensitivity,

- communication and self-advocacy skills related to accommodation needs,
- support surrounding school-related dysregulation and burnout.

Throughout our sessions, [Client Name] has described significant difficulty regulating within environments perceived as sensory-overwhelming or invalidating of [their/his/her] neurodivergent support needs. These difficulties have contributed to emotional distress, functional impairment, and challenges consistently engaging in therapeutic regulation strategies.

A recurring theme within treatment has been [Client Name]'s reported experience of inconsistent accommodation across settings (such as [e.g., open-plan office spaces / unstructured classroom environments]). [Client Name] reports feeling significantly more emotionally regulated in environments where sensory accommodations, direct communication styles, and regulation breaks are predictably integrated. Conversely, [they report / he reports / she reports] increased distress and cognitive overload in settings where these needs are minimized or challenged.

In my clinical opinion, consistent implementation of neurodivergent-affirming support mechanisms across [caregiving/educational/workplace] environments is critical for [Client Name's] emotional regulation and therapeutic progress. Ongoing exposure to invalidating or sensory-overwhelming environments is likely to contribute to continued dysregulation and hinder progress toward treatment goals. At this time, the client would likely benefit from the following:

- consistent sensory accommodations across environments (e.g., noise reduction tools, flexible seating, scheduled regulation breaks),
- reduced exposure to unnecessary sensory overload,
- collaborative communication between caregivers, support staff, and educators regarding regulation strategies,
- continued access to therapeutic support focused on emotional regulation, sensory processing, and coping skills development.

If you require further insight regarding this letter, please contact me using the information below.

Sincerely,

[Clinician Name, Credentials]

[Contact Information]

Worksheet: My Adaptive Tools for Sensory Dysregulation

Instructions: List tools you have used for coping with sensory dysregulation either recently or in the past.

-
-
-
-
-
-
-
-
-
-
-
-
-
-
-

Sensory Dysregulation Accommodation Plan

This report is written by [Clinician Name], and is an accommodation suggestion plan based on psychotherapy sessions with [Client Name]. These recommendations were discussed with the client and are consistent with current clinical knowledge of sensory dysregulation. Please note that this plan is not a formal diagnosis, but rather a plan for therapeutic, home-use, and use by other professionals to evaluate appropriate accommodations.

Name of Client: [Client Name]

Age of Client: [Client Age]

Client's Sensory Considerations:

Accommodations at Home:

- List accommodations here

Accommodations at School:

- List accommodations here

Accommodations in Medical settings:
- List accommodations here

Accommodations in Public:
- List Accommodations here

Accommodations during Travel:
- List accommodations here

Plan in the event of meltdown, shutdown, and burnout:

Assistive Devices for Sensory Dysregulation

In this section, I will mention assistive devices and tools that are commonly helpful for persons struggling with sensory dysregulation; however, this list is not exhaustive and clinicians and persons with sensory dysregulation should be aware that these tools are highly specific to the individual. Many of these coping tools are based on an eclectic approach including sensory-regulation, mindfulness, narrative therapy, and more.

Assistive devices/tools for sensory dysregulation

- Earplugs
- Noise cancelling headphones or ear buds
- Stress balls
- Hand grippers
- Scents (essential oils, candles, etc.)
- Music player in room (Alexa, CD player, radio, etc.)
- Weighted blankets, vests, and other weighted objects.
- Journal (to write down thoughts/sensory stimuli)
- Meditation apps or audiobooks
- Chewable bracelets, necklaces, etc.

- Fidget toys

It is my view that assistive devices for sensory dysregulation are an *adaptive* coping mechanism. Since sensory dysregulation is not a psychological phenomenon, it is important to consider physiological ways to cope as well as tools to help the body self-regulate during these moments. Since sensory information is cumulative, I see no reason to limit these devices and frequently work with clients from a CBT perspective to encourage their use and tackle any personal thought patterns or behaviours that are preventing the use of these devices. The one caveat I have is that any devices that involve hearing (earbuds, earphones) should be set to safe listening levels to decrease the risk of hearing damage.

I have also found both with clients and in my own experience with sensory dysregulation that having access to numerous assistive devices and coping tools can lead to a decrease in anticipatory anxiety and an overall increase in quality of life in the moments where distressing sensory stimuli is not present. Knowing that you have the *option* to use a device or accommodation is often a powerful tool in itself.

Worksheet: Using Adaptive Coping Tools

Instructions: For each distressing sensory stimuli incident, record the date, scenario, coping strategy used, intensity before and after, what worked well, challenges, and lessons learned.

1. **What adaptive tools do you have or could get for coping with sensory dysregulation?**

2. **When do you use adaptive tools?**

3. **How often do you use adaptive tools?**

4. **Are there times you could use adaptive tools but do not? Why?**

5. **Could you implement adaptive tools more?**

6. **Do you think you overuse adaptive tools?**

7. **How do you feel when using adaptive tools?**

8. **Are your thoughts about adaptive tools true?**

9. **When should you use adaptive tools?**

Calming the Nervous System

There are numerous ways to calm your nervous system, many of which involve breathing techniques, going into nature, soothing scents, and practicing meditation. However, there are also strategic sensory tools that can be incorporated. The degree that these coping skills work for sensory dysregulation depends on the person utilizing them. The problem with calming the sensory diverse nervous system is that if you are still in the room with your distressing sensory stimuli, each time you experience the stimuli you will be re-engaging the fight-flight-freeze process.

While this book will offer suggestions for calming the nervous system, it is offered with a caveat: if something does not work for you, or is not enough for a distressing sensory moment, this is not a failure. It is just an unfortunate part of sensory dysregulation that our nervous systems do not habituate to some sensory stimuli and thus we do not *get used to them*. Because of this, the quickest and easiest way to calm the nervous system is to remove the distressing sensory stimuli.

With that in mind, I would suggest finding ways to accommodate sensory dysregulation that involve leaving the room, learning to ask people not to engage in activities that dysregulate you, utilizing devices like noise-cancelling headphones/earplugs, and negotiating accommodations in places that you cannot leave. For some therapists, this can seem counterintuitive as the initial response to *fear* in psychology is usually followed by the idea that you should *never feed the monster* and so you should learn to live in those moments. This, however, is a skill traditionally utilized for PTSD, OCD, and anxiety, rather than sensory dysregulation, which has neurophysiological rather than psychological underpinnings.

People with sensory dysregulation are exposed to their sensory stimuli daily—whether that is chewing, whistling, bright lights, spinning fans, tapping, sneezing, or pen clicking. The stimuli that cause a reaction are everywhere, and they are unavoidable. This is not a phobia where a specific stimulus can be avoided at length. For people with sensory dysregulation, the next sensory stimuli is always creeping around a corner. If exposure cured sensory dysregulation, we would all be sensory dysregulation-free!

Reasonable versus Unreasonable Requests

Perhaps one of the hardest parts of sensory dysregulation is deciding which sensory stimuli should or should not be accommodated by another person. In practice, this is a constant negotiation. This chart is meant to be completed with your partner, family members, or friends. If you and the individual(s) with whom you are writing this list cannot agree if a request is reasonable or unreasonable, then this is an area for further negotiations and discussions around that particular sensory stimulus.

Worksheet: Reasonable versus Unreasonable Requests

Instructions: Decide what requests are reasonable to be accommodated and what requests are not reasonable.

Reasonable Request	Unreasonable Request

Negotiating Boundaries

Unfortunately, there are often sensory stimuli that cannot be avoided by the person with sensory dysregulation. Some sounds, visuals, bright lights, etc. are necessary or unavoidable. More than that, some dysregulating stimuli are part of activities that are important to our partners, parents, friends, etc. This chart is meant to help couples negotiate their "Never", "Sometimes", and "Adapting" sensory stimuli. Adapting stimuli are ones that are necessary or unavoidable. The adapting portion comes in to help negotiate ways for the sensory dysregulation sufferer to live in this environment where distressing sensory stimuli are present. The following example is my own chart based on my own sensory stimuli, but each couple will have a chart tailored to their situations. These categories can change over time! For example, restaurants used to be in my "Never" category. This list should not be treated like scripture, but rather used for neurodivergent individuals and their loved ones to identify their needs and boundaries. Each person with sensory dysregulation will have their own tolerance levels and opinions on these boundaries.

Boundary Negotiation Chart

Never	Sometimes	Adapting

Neurodivergent Therapy

Therapy for neurodivergent and sensory diverse persons should not have the goal of *changing the person* or alleviating the neurotype entirely. Rather than rigid goals like *behaviour adjustments*, persons with neurodivergent brains and bodies must be supported in ways that reflect their own goals and respect their differences. For example, an autistic child should not be 'taught how not to stim' as part of the therapeutic goal, nor should masking one's neurodivergent traits be considered a form of 'treatment'.

Therapy for neurodivergent individuals should be tailored to the individual's needs and their personal concerns. For example, managing emotional regulation, managing anger, learning to cope with sensory distress, helping with suicidal ideation and depression, and coping skills for anxiety. Like with neurotypical persons, therapy should focus on things that are distressing to the individual and their families, and be areas for improvement of one's quality of life, rather than forcing neurotypical ideals on neurodivergent populations.

While the diagnosis of individuals with neurodivergence is helpful for 'treatment', it is not the be-all-and-end-all. Rather, these diverse needs should be taken into account while seeking appropriate interventions. For example, an autistic person may not do well with exposure therapy, even if they have co-occurring conditions where exposure normally helps. For persons who are neurodiverse, their brains and bodies do not necessarily adapt to interventions in the same way as other populations. Diagnosis is a starting point for understanding neurodiverse profiles, and should not be considered as a be-all-and-end-all for providing relief to individuals and families through therapy.

The goals of therapy for persons with neurodivergence must align with their own goals and needs. For example, if a family wants their child to "have more eye contact", "wave their hands less", or "stop pacing around", we are already stepping into the territory of behavioural adjustments and forcing a neurotypical state on a person whose brain and body simply operate differently. By changing these behaviours by coercion, punishment, or 'behavioural therapy', clinicians are perpetuating the dangerous notion that neurodivergent persons need to be fixed. Research shows the exact opposite—masking can lead to neurodivergent burnout, fatigue, sickness, and even suicidality.

Sensory Regulation and Accommodation Plans

Sensory diets are most commonly used in occupational therapy as a way to help persons with sensory needs. However, the use of sensory diets is not limited to a clinical setting and can be used by parents with their children, therapists with their clients, or persons with sensory considerations on their own. The term sensory diet was coined by Patricia and Julia Wilbarger. As described by Susan Nesbit, OT/R, in *Misophonia Matters*:

> The purpose of a Sensory Diet is to use a strategic mix of sensory activities to reduce meltdowns (e.g., yelling or snapping at someone) and shutdowns (withdrawing). Similar to eating food every few hours, the body must be replenished with sensory input. You may need to do a sensory diet every one to two hours. Sensory diets can be used at specific daily time periods or as needed. Choose one or more activities. Doing a sensory diet for 5-15 minutes can be helpful; however, doing a sensory diet for 30 minutes has a longer-lasting effect.

Sensory diets are a structured way to plan for sensory needs and make sensory integration a part of everyday life in a way that is sustainable. Sensory diets should always be led by the individual with sensory needs as they are not like prescriptions—each individual with sensory needs will have their own specific and specialized version of a sensory diet. Sensory diets have been at the core of sensory regulation for several decades; however, in recent years they have become less favourable as some behavioural interventions misuse them by using sensory-based tools and inputs as a punishment or a reward—i.e. "If you do ten jumping jacks then you can have a fidget toy." This is counterintuitive and not within the spirit of sensory regulation or neuroaffirming care.

In my clinical practice, I have transitioned from using sensory diets in their pure form of scheduling sensory input to a more encompassing plan that accounts for both accommodations and sensory regulation. I now use Sensory Regulation and Accommodation Plans and consider them living documents where accommodations and sensory-based skills should be used preventatively, in the moment, and for recovery. By moving away from a strict sensory diet, clients, families, educators, and clinicians can now have a working document that provides an overview of multiple facets of personal management.

Play Therapy

The strengths of play therapy for neurodivergent persons are multifacted—play therapy can help individuals engage in sensory tactile and proprioceptive input, play therapy can foster safety and creativity, and play therapy can be used to navigate emotional dysregulation and safely learn coping skills. Play therapy should be done by professionals who understand the nuance of play and who do not shame neurodivergent persons into an 'appropriate' form of play. It can be a common misconception that some neurodivergent children are playing 'wrong', such as a child lining up their toys and telling stories internally without vocalizing them.

Play therapy is an incredibly neuroaffirming form of therapy that can happen via in-person play, online play such as through digital video games, or even over phone calls or regular sessions where the client merely speaks about their play worlds with the therapist. There is no right or wrong way to do play therapy so long as the client is benefiting from the process in ways that align with therapeutic goals and practice. Clinicians who wish to train in play therapy for neurodivergence, or families looking for practitioners, may be interested in the work of Dr. Robert

Jason Grant called AutPlay, a neurodiversity affirming framework for implementing child and play therapy approaches with neurodivergent children. For more information on incorporating play therapy in a digital environment, I suggest reading the work of Jessica Stone, PhD., especially *Digital Play Therapy.*

Coping Skills You Can Easily Incorporate

Passive coping skills are coping skills that you can incorporate into your life with little to no additional effort. Active coping skills require a little more planning, so they should be chosen carefully. The goal is to choose activities that fit into your life and that do not overwhelm you.

Passive Coping Skills	**Active Coping Skills**
Sleeping with a weighted blanket.	Sew, sculpt clay, do woodworking projects, or scrapbook.
Shower or bath steamers/bombs for scent therapy.	Make a meal involving mixing, chopping, pounding, and so on.
An essential oil diffuser in your room.	Carrying books or other heavy objects across a room or up and down the stairs.
Changing your curtains to a light-blocking style.	Swimming laps.
Wearing a heavy weighted vest.	Switching to taking stairs instead of an elevator.
Listening to coloured noise (e.g., white, pink, and grey).	Going for regular walks, and even better if they are in a calming natural environment.

Fill out your own passive/active coping skills list.

Passive Coping Skills	Active Coping Skills

Physiological Coping Tools

Identifying physiological states can help a person with sensory dysregulation to understand their internal states that can increase the severity of the dysregulated moment. Some of these tools are as follows:

- grounding
- progressive muscle relaxation
- diaphragmatic breathing
- meditation
- mindfulness

Grounding techniques are designed to bring your focus back to the present moment and redirect your attention away from distressing sensory stimuli. When stimuli activate the nervous system, this can lead to a fight-or-flight-or-freeze response, causing you to feel overwhelmed and disconnected from your surroundings. Grounding helps interrupt this cycle by engaging your senses. A common grounding technique is the 5-4-3-2-1 method, where you name five things you can see, four things you can feel, three things you can hear, two things you can smell, and one thing you can taste. This shifts your attention from the distressing stimuli to your immediate environment, helping to calm your nervous system.

Progressive Muscle Relaxation (PMR) is a technique that involves tensing and then relaxing different muscle groups in the body. The goal is to train your body to recognize and release muscle tension which is a common physiological symptom of sensory dysregulation. When a sensory stimulus is present, you may clench your jaw, tighten your shoulders, or tense other muscles without even realizing it. By systematically tensing and relaxing each muscle group (e.g., your hands, arms, neck, shoulders, and legs), you can learn to consciously reduce the physical stress response to distressing sensory stimuli, thereby calming your entire nervous system.

Diaphragmatic breathing, also known as deep belly breathing, is a powerful technique for calming the nervous system. When you are stressed or anxious due to distressing sensory stimuli, your breathing becomes shallow and rapid, which can worsen the fight-or-flight-or-freeze response. Diaphragmatic breathing involves taking slow, deep breaths that engage your diaphragm, slowing your heart rate and lowering your blood pressure. This technique can be practiced by placing one hand on your chest and the other hand on your stomach. As you inhale slowly through your nose, you should feel your belly rise, and as you exhale slowly through your mouth, you should feel it fall. This controlled breathing directly signals your nervous system to relax.

Meditation and mindfulness are intertwined practices that cultivate awareness and a non-judgmental attitude towards your thoughts, feelings, and sensations. The goal is not to eliminate your sensory dysregulation but rather to change your relationship with it. Through mindfulness meditation, you learn to observe sensory stimuli in a less aversive way (although you cannot remove the fight-flight-freeze response entirely). It is the cognitive afterthoughts that we are changing through meditation and mindfulness.

While the above can be helpful for coping with sensory dysregulation, it is important to remember that the needs and wants of the individual are paramount for coping. If a person with sensory dysregulation is averse to any of the above physiological coping skills, then they can be skipped entirely. The goal is not to cause more stress, but rather to adapt to the needs of the individual.

Exercise: Grounding (5-4-3-2-1 Technique)

Instructions: The next time distressing sensory stimuli make you feel overwhelmed, use this exercise to shift your focus back to the present moment and calm your nervous system.

See: Look around and name five things you can see right now.

Feel: Name four things you can physically feel.

Hear: Name three things you can hear (unrelated to the sensory stimuli).

Smell: Name two things you can smell.

Taste: Name one thing you can taste.

Exercise: Progressive Muscle Relaxation

Instructions: Find a comfortable spot to sit or lie down. Consciously tense each muscle group for five seconds, and then completely release the tension as you breathe out.

Hands and Arms: Make a tight fist, and then relax your fingers and let your hands hang loose.

Face: Squeeze your eyes shut and clench your jaw, and then release all the muscles in your face.

Shoulders and Neck: Hunch your shoulders towards your ears, and then let them drop.

Stomach and Chest: Take a deep breath and tighten your stomach muscles, and then exhale and relax.

Legs and Feet: Flex your feet, pulling your toes towards your body, and then release and let them fall.

Exercise: Diaphragmatic Breathing

Instructions: This exercise helps regulate your heart rate and calm your nervous system. Place one hand on your chest and the other hand on your stomach.

Inhale: Breathe in slowly through your nose for a count of four, feeling your stomach expand.

Hold: Hold your breath for a count of two.

Exhale: Breathe out slowly through your mouth for a count of six, feeling your stomach contract.

Repeat this cycle several times until you feel a sense of calm.

Exercise: Mindfulness and Meditation

Instructions: Find a quiet, comfortable space. Set a timer for five minutes. The goal is to observe, not react.

Observe: Acknowledge any misophonic sounds that arise. Silently say to yourself, “There is a sound,” or “I am hearing that sound again.”

Notice Sensations: Pay attention to any physical sensations the sound causes in your body, like a clenched jaw or a tightening in your chest.

Let Go: Gently redirect your focus back to the simple act of breathing.

Repeat: When your mind wanders or you get caught up in a reaction, just notice it and calmly return your attention to your breath.

Worksheet: Physiological Checklist

Instructions: Answer each question to assess your current physiological state.

Am I hungry?

Am I thirsty?

Am I tired?

Am I hot or cold?

Am I in pain?

Do I have a headache?

Am I stressed over something unrelated?

Am I in an environment I dislike or where I feel uncomfortable?

Exercise: 4-7-8 Breathing Technique

Instructions: Follow the activity below to calm your nervous system.

In today's busy world, sensory stimuli sounds often feel unavoidable. Fortunately, there are simple techniques that can help to calm the mind and body. One such method is the 4-7-8 breathing technique, developed by Dr. Andrew Weil and inspired by ancient yogic practices, this technique regulates the nervous system through controlled breath cycles.

How to Practice the 4-7-8 Breathing Technique

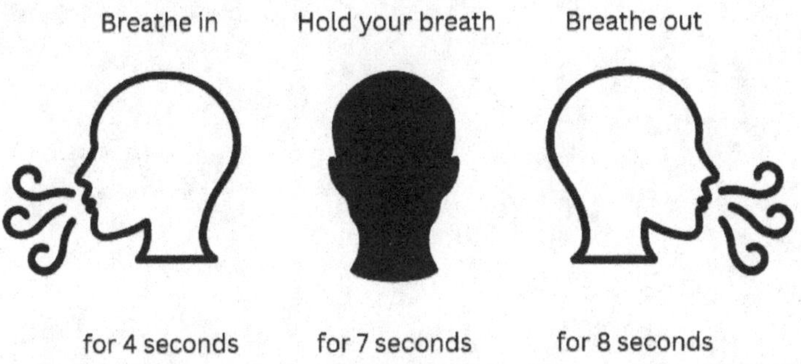

The 4-7-8 breathing method follows these easy steps:

1. Inhale deeply through your nose for 4 seconds.
2. Hold your breath for 7 seconds.
3. Exhale slowly and fully through your mouth for 8 seconds.
4. Repeat as necessary.

This counts as one full cycle, and beginners are encouraged to repeat it up to four times. With consistent practice, many people experience noticeable relaxation after just a few rounds.

When to Use This Technique

The 4-7-8 breathing exercise can be practiced anytime you feel stressed, anxious, or overwhelmed, whether it is by sensory dysregulation or otherwise.

Worksheet: My Sensory Dysregulation Accommodations

Instructions: Describe past accommodations, their effectiveness, potential future accommodations, and their feasibility.

Have you ever had accommodations for sensory dysregulation?

If so, did they help?

What accommodations do you think could help?

Are these accommodations possible?

Non-Negotiable Coping Skills

Coping with sensory dysregulation is not always easy and is often a challenge. Even somebody with numerous coping skills may find it hard to rely on their coping skills when in fight-flight-freeze mode, have other problems going on, or other health or life issues. However, it can be helpful to have coping skills that are non-negotiable and become the default for sensory dysregulation. By creating these non-negotiable defaults, the idea is that even in fight-flight-freeze mode these coping skills will become a habitual behaviour. Non-negotiable coping skills should not be imposed on the sensory dysregulation sufferer by a therapist, family member, or partner. It is imperative that the sensory dysregulation sufferer has full consent over their coping skills and has decided that they will be using these skills regularly.

Of course, there is always a chance that these coping skills will not work continually or will require necessary adjustments. This should not be considered a failure but rather a part of the process. The idea is to have a set list of coping skills that are always available and at the top of mind. Preparing a sensory dysregulation grab bag for times outside the house and a printed list can be helpful to keep these skills at the top of mind. It can also be useful to print the list and post it on the wall in areas that are frequented.

For myself, I like to consider my "non-negotiable" coping skills as "being my own mom". For example, I would never let my child go hungry, be tired, continue doing a task when overwhelmed or burnt out, or locked in a house without going outside for air. Sometimes it can be hard to treat ourselves with the same amount of attention that we would give to somebody in our care.

Worksheet: Non-Negotiable Coping Skills

Instructions: List your essential, non-negotiable coping skills for managing sensory dysregulation.

-
-
-
-
-
-
-
-
-
-

Avoidance of Using Coping Mechanisms

The avoidance of using accommodations or assistive devices for sensory dysregulation is something that often arises in my clinical practice. Clients across different age groups have reported similar resistance to using coping mechanisms that have been suggested for sensory dysregulation. Sometimes this resistance is due to cognitive reasons, and other times there are physical reasons such as discomfort and headaches or another condition which limits mobility or accessibility.

Common reasons for not using sensory dysregulation accommodations and devices include, but are not limited to, the following:

- Belief that the people making the distressing sensory stimuli are justified in doing so.
- Resentment that accommodations and tools should not be necessary and are unfair.
- Discomfort with using devices such as earplugs and headphones due to physical reasons (dislike how they feel, head pressure, etc.).
- Physical disability (inability to go for walks, inability to easily change environments, etc.).

- Embarrassment or worry that others will judge the use of accommodations (if I wear headphones in class people will think I am weird).
- Worry about being perceived as being rude (if I wear earplugs my co-worker will think I am ignoring them).

While not every reason for avoiding accommodations is dictated by controllable factors, by focusing on views and beliefs that *can be changed*, there is room to increase adherence to coping mechanisms and thus lower the overall distress of sensory dysregulation. It is important to focus on what *can be changed* rather than what *cannot be*.

Worksheet: Remembering Coping Skills

Instructions: Create a list of reminders for adaptive coping tools and activities for sensory dysregulation.

-
-
-
-
-
-
-
-
-
-
-
-

Ongoing Support and Community

A great deal of systemic support for persons with sensory dysregulation and forms of neurodivergence does not provide support after the most socially challenging and disruptive symptoms are either alleviated or dealt with in a way that is more palpable for an institutional neurotypical framework.

Even mental health workers and psychotherapists and occupational therapists are often convinced by their peers that there should be an end date to services and that support is a crutch rather than a life-long part of coping with neurodivergence. I completely reject this idea and believe that we need therapeutic support, community support, and peer support that is ongoing and not conditional on meeting arbitrary 'markers' of success.

Local support groups, online groups, and therapeutic groups that are less formal but led by a clinician can all help to provide ongoing access to support to assist neurodivergent individuals as new challenges arise. Living with neurodivergence is not something to be 'treated' and then pushed back into the world. If we are truly serious about helping neurodivergent individuals, we will have ongoing community, therapeutic, and institutional support and advocacy.

Conclusion

The goal this book hopes to achieve is to introduce the world of sensory diversity, sensory dysregulation, and a neuroaffirming framework. It is my hope that the sections within provide clarity and understanding regarding sensory dysregulation, and that this text serves as merely the beginning of the conversation. For those who live with sensory dysregulation, these challenges exist across multiple facets of daily life; my goal is for this book to serve as both a tool for personal coping skills and a work of ongoing advocacy.

I would like to close on the note that sensory diversity is a transdiagnostic framework designed to explain the natural variations in sensory processing between different brains—both neurotypical and neurodivergent alike.

Excerpt from

Misophonia Matters

An Advocacy-Based Approach to Coping with Misophonia for Adults and Clinicians
by Shaylynn Hayes-Raymond

What is Misophonia?

"What is Misophonia?" is one of the most contentious questions that I have ever dealt with. If you ask some, it is a psychiatric condition where people are overreacting to stimuli. I do not believe this. For me, misophonia is atypical neurological processing of audial and visual information (Kumar et al., 2017). However, it remains a contentious question. The disorder continues to make people's lives worse, and yet we cannot land on a definition of what it is exactly.

To me, misophonia is the worst thing that has ever happened to me. Misophonia is a condition which means that every part of my life is now a negotiation. From a purely emotional and life-based perspective, misophonia is a constant flux of negotiating triggers and the possibility of triggers. No amount of scientific debate takes away the fact that misophonia is something that causes great suffering and pain to those who have it.

Scientifically, I believe that misophonia is a neurophysiological disorder where otherwise non-aversive stimuli cause a fight-flight-freeze reaction (Brout et al., 2018), yet that does not say very much when it comes to the everyday lives of those with misophonia. As scientists argue in academic articles about *what part of the brain* is impacted by misophonia and as they do treatment studies which turn out to have essentially placebo levels of treatment (and yet tote them as "helpful"), we are still here with this condition wondering… what exactly this condition is that is akin to our own personal hell.

Research and understanding of misophonia are new in the grand scheme of neuroscience and psychology. The term misophonia was first coined in 2001 when audiologists Drs. Jastreboff and Jastreboff discovered that there was a differentiation in their practice between tinnitus, hyperacusis, and misophonia patients (Jastreboff and Jastreboff, 2001). The culture surrounding misophonia is one of online support groups and websites which band together to help researchers understand their condition and share their commonalities to fill in the gaps of a literature that has yet to fully conceptualize or honor their experiences. Some of these communities include the use of social media communities, internet websites, or nonprofits which advocate for sufferers with the disorder. Misophonia sufferers often consider themselves "misophones" in their communities, and they are very vocal about research and stigma surrounding their disorder (Misophonia International, n.d.). Persons with misophonia are often upset by the prospect of exposure therapy, and feel that if exposure worked, they would all be cured as there is no way to fully limit exposure to otherwise normal sensory stimuli such as coughing, chewing, whistling, and pen tapping.

Although misophonia is in its infancy as a recognized disorder, it has been shown to be "associated with altered brain activity in the auditory cortex and salience network" (Schröder et al., 2019), as well as having a brain basis including the sensory motor system (Kumar et al., 2017; 2021). Research has found that the amount of exposure does not change the emotional response to misophonia and thus exposure therapy would not be an effective form of treatment (Rosenthal et al., 2022). One study showed that persons with misophonia share similar traits to those with autism (Rinaldi et al., 2023), further justifying the use of a sensory regulation-based approach to misophonia. Accommodations for misophonia have also been shown to be beneficial in a school environment, and thus could be similarly useful in a workplace environment (Porcaro et al., 2019). There have been some statistical findings suggesting that CBT can be helpful for misophonia (Jager et al., 2021); however, the community's perceptions of CBT and differentiating between types of CBT are important when moving forward with any client. For example, some CBT helps people to change their beliefs about a trigger and learn to live in a world with that trigger, whereas other practitioners might try exposure therapy and there is no one size fits all for CBT. It is important when treating and conceptualizing misophonia to remember how "To date, no randomized controlled trials evaluating treatments for misophonia have been published" (Brout et al., 2018).

What is Sensory Processing Disorder?

By Susan Nesbit, M.S., OT.

In the 1960s, Dr. Ayres described Sensory Integration Dysfunction (SID), including tactile defensiveness (Ayres, 1968; 1972; 1979). She suggested that children who overreact to touch (e.g., they do not like getting their hair and nails cut, will not wear certain textures of clothes, and avoid activities such as finger painting) have a protective tactile system that is always on. The discriminative tactile system (e.g., knowing that you are feeling your keys in the bottom of your purse without looking at them) is not overriding the protective tactile system, and the unimportant tactile information does not get filtered out. With the bombardment of protective tactile information, a child with tactile defensiveness is in a pattern of fight-or-flight (e.g., they are unable to sit still and feel the keys in their hands). Dr. Ayres further proposed that activities with deep pressure (e.g., hugging and jumping) enable the discriminative tactile system to override the protective tactile system so the unimportant tactile information can be filtered out and the child can be available for learning.

Imagine a child with tactile defensiveness playing on a seesaw. The seat with the protective tactile system (sympathetic nervous system) stays up, causing the child to flail (to wildly swing their arms and legs) with anger and other negative emotions. The seat with the discriminative tactile system (parasympathetic nervous system) does not go up, so the child is unable to enjoy the seesaw. Children need to balance the seesaw by alternating the seat for the protective tactile system going up (so they can run if they see a fire) with the seat for the discriminative tactile system going up (so they can sit still without flailing, and they can have fun and learn in a safe environment).

In the 1980s, other scholars proposed that defensiveness exists in other sensory channels, and several other types of sensory defensiveness were labeled and described, including auditory (sounds), visual (sights), and olfactory (smell). Because the protective and the discriminative tactile systems address only tactile defensiveness, and not defensiveness in the other sensory channels, the more recent scholars theorized that the amygdala is the filter, with the inhibitory fibers not overriding the excitatory fibers. The excitatory fibers are constantly firing, thereby letting in unimportant information so a person is wired for fight, flight, or freeze. The sympathetic and the parasympathetic nervous systems are unbalanced. These scholars suggested using activities that provide deep pressure and slow linear movement to help the inhibitory fibers override the excitatory fibers.

Moving into the twenty-first century, Dr. Lucy Jane Miller coined the terminology commonly used today. Sensory Integration Disorder is now referred to as a Sensory Processing Disorder (SPD) (Miller et al., 2009; 2021), which is an umbrella term with three primary diagnostic categories: (a) Sensory Modulation Disorder (SMD), (b) Sensory Discrimination Disorder (SDD), and Sensory-Based Motor Disorder (SBMD). Each diagnostic category has subtypes.

SMD has three subtypes: (a) Sensory Over-Responsivity (SOR), (b) Sensory Under-Responsivity (SUR), and Sensory Craving (SC). Persons can have SOR, SUR, and/or SC in one or more of the various sensory channels. Sensory channels include the following: auditory (sounds), visual (sights), tactile (touch), pain (physical distress), olfactory (smells), gustatory (tastes), proprioception/vestibular (position/movement), air temperature (hot or cold), and interoception (e.g., hunger pangs). Persons with SOR perceive the input from one or more of the sensory channels as noxious, harmful, or threatening. For example, a child with an auditory over-responsivity might cover their ears when someone whistles or jangles their keys. In contrast, persons with SUR barely perceive the input from one or more of the sensory channels. For example, a child with bumps and bruises might feel minimal pain. And a person with SC seeks input from one or more of the sensory channels. Examples include a child touching and/or smelling objects as they walk through a room, a child who seeks movement having difficulty sitting still, and a child who seeks proprioceptive input (pressure) intentionally bumping into things, including people.

SDD has six subtypes: (a) Auditory, (b) Visual, (c) Tactile, (d) Taste/Smell, (e) Position/Movement, and (f) Interoception.

SBMD has two subtypes: Dyspraxia and Postural Disorder. Persons with dyspraxia (poor motor planning) have problems doing new or unfamiliar tasks such as learning to tie shoelaces. They do not learn to tie their shoelaces automatically (without thinking), and when they feel stressed, the task of tying is even more challenging.

Postural disorders include poor balance and low muscle tone.

Misophonia and auditory over-responsivity might overlap. (Note: SPD is used interchangeably with the term auditory over-responsivity. To be in sync with others, I will use the term SPD when referring to a sensory modulation disorder, including auditory over-responsivity.)

Misophonia is a strong dislike or hatred of specific sounds. Persons with misophonia dislike soft or loud repetitive sounds, especially sounds made by the mouth. Triggers include chomping food, slurping a drink, snapping gum, humming, and whistling. Other triggers include opening a bag of chips, cracking knuckles, and texting with the volume on. Sounds are not triggers when the person with misophonia makes them. Sounds are triggers when another person makes them.

When exposed to a trigger, people with misophonia feel anger, disgust, and hate. In contrast, people with hyperacusis feel pain from loud and/or high-pitched sounds such as sirens and alarms, screeching brakes on subways or buses, silverware clanking against dishes, children's screams, and clapping. Some loud repetitive triggers overlap with the triggers for misophonia. For example, silverware clanking against dishes is listed as a trigger for each condition.

People with SPD dislike all of the above sounds. The emotional manifestations (anger, disgust, and hate) and the behaviors (fight, flight, or freeze) of persons with misophonia and SPD seem similar.

Some persons diagnosed with misophonia are reported to have visual sensitivities in addition to their auditory sensitivities. The term misokinesia has been used to mean a hatred of movement. People with misokinesia strongly dislike seeing movements such as someone twirling their hair around and around their finger, someone moving their legs up and down while sitting, and someone chewing food or gum with their open mouth.

Persons with SPD typically have problems in more than one sensory channel; therefore, over-responsiveness to inputs such as visual and tactile in addition to auditory over-responsivity suggest SPD. However, the auditory sensory channel might be the only sense affected in SPD. Therefore, the question of whether misophonia and SPD are linked needs to be investigated. Please bear in mind that the current lack of research does not rule out a potential link between these two conditions.

SPD is thought to be a neurodevelopmental condition, meaning that it is a disorder within the brain that affects emotions, self-control, attention/memory, and learning throughout the lifespan. Research is ongoing; however, the neurobiological mechanisms and the implicated structures in the brain are poorly documented. The etiologies (causes) are unknown, but a genetic vulnerability is possible in some persons with SPD. Fewer studies exist for misophonia. Whether this condition is neurological or learned from experiences is controversial. Research is needed to investigate the similarities and the differences between SPD and misophonia and to investigate the possible co-occurrence of these conditions.

The potential exists that some persons have been misdiagnosed, and an incorrect diagnosis could lead to the wrong treatments, which could worsen the symptoms. The causes of misophonia and SPD could be different. Causes guide treatments; therefore, research to find the causes for misophonia and SPD is important.

Occupational therapists evaluate for SPD with informal tests, such as observations and interviews, and with formal tests that are standardized for validity and reliability. Formal tests include the Sensory Profiles and the Sensory Processing Measures. These two batteries of tests use age-appropriate and environmentally appropriate (home versus classroom) forms.

Occupational therapists have been treating children and adults diagnosed with Sensory Integration Disorder (SID), now called Sensory Processing Disorder (SPD), since the 1960s. Some people come for intervention in a sensory gym with a variety of swings, climbing structures, balls, bolsters (rolls), mats, and other equipment to provide body movement and proprioception (deep pressure). The other sensory systems are treated as well. For example, sensory bins are used for persons with tactile problems.

Occupational therapists work with students in schools, giving teachers suggestions to help students with SPD stay on task. Suggestions include providing movement by sending the student on errands such as taking the class attendance to the office and/or allowing them to sharpen pencils; providing movement while sitting by using a wobble chair or a standard chair with a wobble cushion;

providing pressure against the student's torso (trunk) by allowing them to sit backwards in their chair; providing movement and pressure on different body parts by allowing the student to switch positions (e.g., alternating between a sitting position—including sitting on their legs, a standing position, and stomach lying on the carpet); and providing structured fidgeting by allowing the student to rub their hand(s) across Velcro taped inside the top of a desk, twist the pieces at the top of a fidget pencil, play with a fidget toy, and/or press their feet against the legs of their desk.

Occupational therapists also work with parents, giving home programs with sensory activities and making suggestions for modifying (changing) the home environment. The goals of classroom and home modifications are to reduce the number of noxious stimuli and to provide ways to stay calm or regain composure when triggered.

SPD has no cure. However, the symptoms can be temporarily lessened through a variety of treatments, including sensory diets. Similar to a diet of food, the input from a sensory diet does not last indefinitely in the body. The input lasts one to two hours, or less when stressed by noxious stimuli.

Sensory diets include activities for pressure and movement. Activities can include hiking, walking, or running; doing animal walks (e.g., elephant, bear, rabbit, frog, duck, and crab); wheelbarrow walking; floor or chair pushups; "play" wrestling; bouncing on a hopper ball (they come in adult sizes); jumping (e.g., up and down with both legs together or jumping jacks) on the floor or a mini-trampoline (use a regular trampoline if one is available); playing on a variety of swings, climbing structures, and slides; doing yoga (classes and books/flash cards are available for adults and children); using fidget toys; manipulating Play-Doh or modeling clay; and coloring mandalas (beginning at the center). Doing heavy work, including taking out the garbage, mowing the lawn, carrying the laundry, and pushing furniture to vacuum, can be included in a sensory diet.

I am a pediatric occupational therapist, and I have misophonia and SPD. To avoid becoming overwhelmed by triggers, I control my environment as much as possible. For example, I ask people not to whistle or crack their knuckles. I leave the room if someone is chomping food. I have been called controlling; however, the alternative is melting down or shutting down.

When initially triggered, I typically remain calm. I can think and be proactive. I can stay calm until the frequency (number) of the triggers increases, the intensity (strength) of just one trigger increases, and/or the duration (length of time) of just one trigger extends. When the triggers accumulate, I become overwhelmed.

When I become overwhelmed, I am unable to think and I become reactive. I have an “adult” meltdown by snapping at the person whom I view to be noxious or by crying. I try to reserve my crying until I am alone, but I am not always successful. If I do not have a meltdown, then I shut down (withdraw) and I do not listen.

I can become overwhelmed with sound triggers alone, but with the addition of other triggers—sights, smells, being hot, and/or being hungry—I more easily become overwhelmed and I have a bigger meltdown or I withdraw more deeply. I experience what I call the “additive effect”, which I will describe later in a different section.

For people with SPD, and possibly with misophonia, I suggest using a sensory diet (examples given above). When I am unable to leave the negative situation to do some of the activities such as walking, I hug myself by squeezing my torso with my arms crossed, and I cross my legs at my knees and my ankles (I am flexible). Sometimes I clasp my hands together and squeeze—under the table when possible—I try to be inconspicuous. (Note: I have successfully explained to social workers and psychologists who work with persons with SPD that by crossing my arms around my body and by crossing my legs, I am not communicating that I am closed to them and not listening. Instead, through the pressure provided in these positions, I can remain calm to listen.)

I also try to reframe my negative thoughts by thinking about something positive, e.g., this meeting will be over in 15 minutes and then I will get a gourmet coffee. Sometimes, sounds that I enjoy mingle with sounds that I hate, and I try to focus on the sounds that I enjoy. For example, if someone is triggering me on the NYC subway, I will try to listen to the wheels moving along the tracks. Sometimes I visualize walking in a forest surrounded by the sounds that I love (e.g., a waterfall gliding over the rocks into a pond, the rustle of the pine needles under my feet, and the singing birds perched in the trees). I visualize watching the white fluffy clouds moving across the cerulean-blue sky. I stop to smell the roses. I feel the rain on my skin. Sometimes I breathe deeply, counting as I inhale and exhale. Sometimes I progressively relax my muscles. But when I am tipped over the edge and I cannot think, visualizing the triggering person getting run over by a tractor-trailer truck is helpful. (Note: reframing, mindfulness, visualization, deep breathing, and progressive muscle relaxation work for me only when the triggers are few, not intense, and not lasting a long time.)

Sensory information accumulates. Imagine a set of triggers: You are at a low level of arousal and your alarm clock rings. You push the snooze button and it goes off again in only 5 minutes and you are still tired. You get out of bed and step on a toy. You go to make coffee and discover that you have no cream. You pick up the cereal box and it opens on the bottom, spilling onto the floor. Your child will not get dressed. You finally leave the house and back your car out of your garage, hitting your child's bicycle. By now, even a person without misophonia or SPD might be on a high level of arousal (sensory overload). Before driving your car, try to take a break to reset your level of arousal from high to normal.

To describe what I call the additive effect, I will use my auditory and visual triggers in a mathematical equation.

I will give a score of 2 (for mathematical purposes only; I am not using a scale to rate how much I hate the trigger) to hearing someone chomping their food. And I will give a score of 2 for seeing that person chewing with their mouth open. In this scenario, 2 + 2 does not equal 4. Instead, 2 + 2 equals 5.

When possible, modify your environment to reduce the frequency (number), the intensity (strength), and the duration (length of time) of the triggers. Modifying the environment is helpful for persons with misophonia and/or SPD.

For people with SPD, I gave examples of activities for a sensory diet in an earlier section. Identify the sensory activities that work best for you. Do a sensory diet for 5-10 minutes. Because the sensory activities are part of a diet, you may need to do them every one or two hours. You may need to do them more often if triggered. Another easy-to-do technique is self-hugging, as described in an earlier question.

Bear in mind that if the cause of misophonia is different than the cause of SPD, then a sensory diet may not be effective for misophonia. Some scholars speculate, however, that misophonia also could be neurologically based, and perhaps the same structures in the central nervous system (the brain) are involved.

If you live with a person with misophonia or SPD, I suggest allowing that person to have control, or at least perceived control, to create a structured and supportive environment. By perceived control, I mean giving choices; however, every choice is acceptable to you. In an example: You need to do two errands and take your child along. You know that they dislike hearing noises in stores. You can give them the choice of which store they would like to go to first. You can say, "I know you hate shopping (empathy); however, we need to shop for dinner and buy daddy a new hammer. Which store would you like to go to first? The grocery store or the hardware store?" You are setting limits with two acceptable choices. You also can solve problems together by asking them how they can cope (be less angry) with the noise. Bear in mind that persons with misophonia and SPD are controlling in an effort to reduce triggers (noxious stimuli) to prevent sensory overload.

Our Voices and Needs

The entire concept of *Misophonia Matters* is drawn from the idea that no one understands misophonia more than the people who have misophonia. Whether you are reading this as a sufferer of misophonia, or a clinician who is working with those with misophonia, the important takeaway is that misophonia is a complex condition that is poorly understood.

Although it was nearly a decade ago, I remember like it was yesterday hearing Kathie Lee and Hoda speak about misophonia in a segment. The two talked about the term misophonia, mentioned chewing rage, and then gawked about how the disorder did not sound real—and even called it "misophoney". Dr. Phil berated a person with misophonia on his show. The press has dubbed misophonia chewing rage and treated sufferers like circus clowns, an amusing population they had never heard of before, ripe for berating. With its status as a lesser-known disorder, many have not yet got the message that mocking persons with misophonia is cruel.

This stigmatization makes it harder for sufferers of the disorder to feel safe explaining their condition to loved ones, employers, school staff, and other important individuals in their lives. Stigma is more than something we internalize, it shapes the way one interacts with the world, and can impact the level of support and understanding that an individual receives. Numerous misophonia sufferers have exclaimed to me upon learning that there is a name for the disorder, "Oh my god, I thought I was just crazy!" This pervasive view that sufferers of misophonia are strange, crazy, or overreacting is one that I hope shifts through advocacy and public awareness.

The State of Misophonia Research

Misophonia research is something that I have found perplexing in my years of advocacy. As a person who does believe in the scientific process, I understand why theories need to be proven and disproven. What I do not understand is why researchers are constantly ignoring the information that has been presented to them by sufferers of the very disorder they are researching.

As more and more studies start to come out on misophonia, I am finding it hard to understand why some of these studies exist. For example, some studies have questioned whether or not *misophonia should be accommodated*, or whether or not misophonia is something that is psychiatric, or whether or not misophonia should be treated with exposure therapy or behavioral interventions. This is all despite years of sufferers of misophonia speaking out about how their therapists and clinicians have *already been trying these treatments* to no avail, and in some cases, causing more distress than before "treatment".

Of course, we need studies on *why* things do not work. After all, I cannot cite to you *why* exposure therapy for misophonia is cruel and unhelpful, yet at this point I think it is important that we do not ignore the perceptions of people with misophonia who have already been treated by therapists with exposure therapy. If these forms of therapy worked, do you not think that *somebody* would have said so? There are hundreds of thousands of people with misophonia on the internet, yet you would be hard-pressed to find a support group that supports the concept of exposure therapy. Are these voices not important to the design of a study for misophonia?

Much of this was the ethos of starting The International Misophonia Foundation, a non-profit registered in Missouri dedicated to misophonia and sensory processing disorders. If those who have misophonia are not included in the design of research, then the research might never reflect our actual values and experiences. It is one thing to collect data from individuals with misophonia and come to conclusions. It is another thing entirely for the design of the research to always have the community in mind.

I recently had a conversation with a notable researcher in the misophonia community who responded to a petition in favor of misophonia accommodations by telling me that accommodations are "counterproductive, hinders effective treatment, and if it is at the high level it prevents success". To me this is a strange claim since we do not have an effective treatment for misophonia to hinder. How do you hinder something that has yet to actually exist? I am also unsure what level of success could be stopped by accommodations, particularly since most people with misophonia simply want to live their lives without feeling grueling torture.

If researchers are worried that overaccommodating will lead to unrealistic expectations of the world, I think that is fair, but I counter the point by saying that alleviating your suffering in some aspects of your life can make your quality of life better overall, and then your nervous system is less taxed and more able to handle the bad situations as they come.

The opposite of accommodations would be to desensitize to the sounds. If this worked, I think all of us would be cured because most triggers for misophonia are ever-present. This is not some phobia where we can avoid the stimuli and live our lives sheltered from fear. Everyday sounds (and visuals) are causing us great distress, and the longer our nervous systems are taxed, the worse we feel. For example, after a long day of being triggered I will simply shut down and no longer be able to think properly or respond. I practically feel catatonic, and then I get a migraine and feel sick.

We also need to stop ignoring decades of sensory processing disorder research that talks about using interoception and proprioception to lower arousal, rather than simply looking for random solutions where they do not need to exist. The willful blindness of researchers to ignore over 40 years of relevant research is frustrating, to say the least. Auditory over responsivity was not a new phenomenon before being carelessly named misophonia in 2001, but now we are doing new research without any heading, completely disregarding the work of Jean Ayres, Lucy Miller, Teresa May Benson, and other sensory researchers. Let us stop pretending that there is no research to look at and actually start talking to other researchers. Everybody wants to be the one to "cure" misophonia, and in the meantime, they are making suggestions that actively harm our communities. Enough is enough.

An effective treatment for misophonia does not exist. If we knew about it, then we would gladly share it. Therefore, what treatments are accommodations making less effective? I am unsure how it could, since the disorder is in a preliminary stage of investigation. Yet, what we do know is that the quality of life of these very real people is made better by making adjustments to their environment. All these researchers are doing is adding more shame and stigma to an already misunderstood phenomenon. We are struggling enough… let me keep my headphones, my earplugs, and my ability to leave the room!

Since misophonia is a newly described disorder, and one for which a consensus is still being reached, there is much room for researchers to get things wrong. In fact, getting things wrong is often an important part of the scientific approach. This is why replication is one of the most important things in studies—if something cannot be replicated, it is not yet seen as truth. And yet, despite this, charlatans are often quick to tote "studies" (often singular case studies without replication) as "proof" that their treatment or theory is legitimate. This is dangerous.

I want to first point out that technically speaking, anybody can be published as a researcher. Traditional barriers of entry like having a research center or university backing are becoming less and less important with the birth of entirely online journals. More chillingly, there is a growing number of *pay to play* publications that essentially take the money of the author—go through an expedited "peer review" process—and then churn out whatever "research" was submitted under the guise of science. There is no money in rejecting numerous papers. This is why people who do not have graduate degrees or even clinical backgrounds can get into so many journals. Whether a person is a nurse, a doctor, or a journalist, their "research" can join the world with little to no barriers. Except, of course, a little money.

To further this unethical practice, the internet has little to no rules for claims and name ownership. One can be an "institute" or a "center" without ever having a physical address or license to back this claim. After all, anybody can buy a domain name with a tricky keyword and try to tell the world they are an expert. This is a frustrating reality, but one we have to live with and learn to parse and avoid for ourselves.

Even more insidious than pay to play researchers are doctorate level researchers without sufficient neuroscience background insisting that misophonia is cognitive. This is particularly pervasive with CBT research, despite little to no replicable evidence that exposure therapy or CBT is helpful for misophonia. In fact, most people with misophonia who tried exposure techniques have come back saying it was a "torturous" experience. With that said, these cognitive researchers are so shut off and set in their ways that they refuse to acknowledge research from neuroscientists like Sukhbinder Kumar (2017; 2021) which shows an entirely different picture of misophonia—and one that has been verified with brain scans, not just with case studies and conjecture.

It is very unfortunate that even at the doctorate level we have researchers who are ignoring emerging studies and toting their own irresponsible theories as scientific evidence. Even more insidious, these researchers have easier access to publication and are well-respected by their peers. I am horrified by the possibility that cognitive behavioral therapy (CBT), and more concerningly exposure therapy, will become the go-to approach for therapists worldwide merely because of half-baked research that presents misophonia as receptive to exposure—despite little evidence that it is cognitive instead of neurological.

This is flabbergasting to me. I was always taught that science is the pursuit of following the evidence, but instead, many camps of theories are emerging that are blatantly ignoring the reality, data, and brain scans of people who actually have misophonia and were studied.

Parents and sufferers must be proactive about misophonia advocacy. It is an unfortunate reality that we must be vigilant when we read "scientific" studies, but like science itself, questioning everything and seeing if there are replicated results (multiple sources) is the only way forward.

Almost every researcher on the planet would like to stand up and say that they care more about research than they do about their own ego and their own perspective on their research. I would argue that every single one of them, even the most noble and most ethical among them, is wrong. Ego is central to human experience. We appreciate our work because we believe in it, and when you spend years, and often decades, in a field, you are bound to have grown emotionally attached to your work. This becomes a problem when egos get in the way of new research, but more insidiously, of researchers who omit other studies and researchers because by speaking of their peers more often, their peers gain greater recognition.

Grants and funding are central in the research world. Notoriety and publishing credits all go toward your ability to generate funds. With this in mind, a researcher may be cautious at reaching out to a fellow expert. If that expert has *more papers than them* on a subject, this further bolsters the image of their competition. In a perfect world, there would be no competition, only good ideas, and experts working together to further the research and understanding of misophonia. And yet, we do not live in a perfect world, and probably never will.

What can be done about this? It is important that researchers are aware of other studies and are not omitting citations or perspectives on their work that paint a fuller picture of disorders, and yet, we know this happens every day across all scientific disciplines. In some cases, this may not even be professional self-interest, but a more stringent view which does not allow for reflection on cross-disciplinary studies. I am looking at you, behaviorally focused or cognitively focused groups. I am also not attacking one particular researcher. It is a grueling endeavor to finish a bachelor's degree, then a master's degree, and then an additional five or so years of doctoral study only to have to fight tooth and nail for a scrap of funding for your studies. At this point, I am sure that only gluttons for punishment are researchers because the field is so unkind and unforgiving to its dedicated members.

I think many of the problems lie with how research is funded at a policy level. Who is funding the research? Are they looking at the substantive picture of the researchers? Or is funding based on some sort of popularity contest?

Guidelines for funding research are spotty at best, and at worst they are a popularity contest. A commitment to scientific study must come from both the funders and the researchers, as well as the community that is impacted by this research. This commitment is one that must be ongoing.

As scientists go around telling the world that the "treatment" for misophonia is cognitive behavioral therapy, I think it is important to note that any findings on CBT that have been seen are akin to that of a coping skill— they help deal with the emotional after-effects of misophonia, not the misophonic moment, and certainly not as a preventative measure. You cannot CBT the misophonia away, and you surely should not be out there referring to CBT as a "treatment" for misophonia. This is a disingenuous move by researchers, clinicians, and those involved in the use of CBT to skew public perception on CBT.

I am not saying that CBT is unhelpful for misophonia. Like all coping skills approaches, there is room for CBT when we are trying to help people with misophonia mitigate the after-effects of the disorder and learn how to live in a world that is not accommodating to their sensory needs. Yet, this does not mean that CBT is the gold standard, and it absolutely does not mean that we should be toting things like exposure therapy. I repeat: if exposure worked, we would all be cured, as none of us can completely ignore stimuli. Misophonia is also not a behavioral disorder. We do not *learn* to hate sounds and we cannot *learn not to*. In fact, saying that misophonia is "hatred of sounds" in general is untrue because there is already proof that there is a brain basis and the amygdala and fight-flight response are involved (Kumar et al., 2017; 2021).

I understand that scientists are using familiar language, but they should be cautious when explaining any cognitive-based, or even sensory-based, skill for misophonia as a "treatment". The very word treatment assumes that misophonia can be mitigated by the skills learned, and that is simply not true. CBT is helpful to take the edge off and learn how to understand misophonia through worksheets and psychoeducation, but that does not mean that it should be referred to as a treatment. In fact, I would wager that calling anything a treatment at this point in time is nothing more than wishful thinking.

Much of the problem, I assume, is the reliance on "treatments" in American medicine and "psychiatric care". The use of insurance codes means that specific interventions must be referred to as treatments in order to be approved for use and reimbursement. Frankly, this entire practice is backwards and wrong, and this is why in places like Canada where I live this is unheard of and it only muddies the waters when it comes to the expectations of those receiving these "treatments". Instead, practitioners and researchers should be honest and explain CBT for what it is, a coping skill for the disorder, and not the gold standard approach to helping sufferers.

Shaylynn Hayes-Raymond is an LCT-C with a MA in Counselling Psychology, BA in Political Science, and honours diploma in Creative Digital Media. Shaylynn is the director of the International Misophonia Foundation and a private-practice therapist in New Brunswick, Canada. Shaylynn has written numerous pieces on misophonia and has been an advocate for the condition since 2014. Shaylynn is the founder of Sensory Diversity, a website and advocacy movement dedicated to educating and providing awareness on the concept of sensory diversity—and through this work, helping those with sensory dysregulation through coping skills and psychoeducation.

www.ingramcontent.com/pod-product-compliance
Lightning Source LLC
LaVergne TN
LVHW030726061126
851857LV00019B/2004